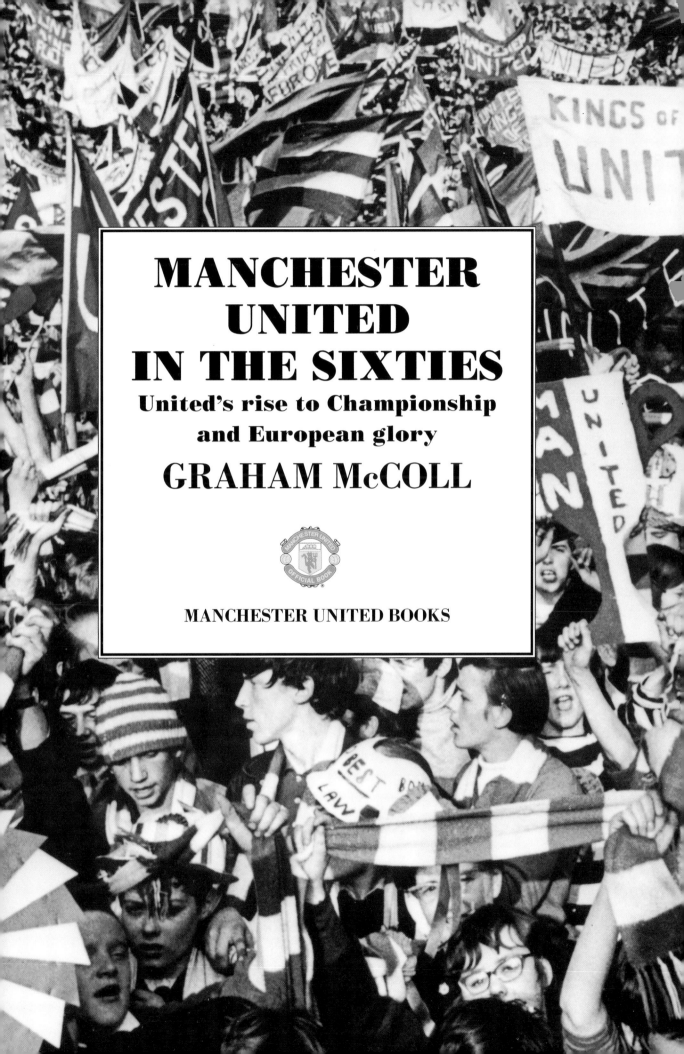

MANCHESTER UNITED IN THE SIXTIES

United's rise to Championship and European glory

GRAHAM McCOLL

MANCHESTER UNITED BOOKS

Author Acknowledgements
I would like to thank Nicky Paris, editor at André Deutsch and Alastair Gourlay, production manager at André Deutsch for suggesting me for the project and for their professionalism under pressure. I would also like to thank Annette Doutney, copy editor and Cliff Butler at Manchester United for their careful reading of the first drafts of the book. The newspaper archive at The Mitchell Library in Glasgow was an invaluable source of research material particularly for back issues of the *Guardian*, *The Times* and the *Glasgow Herald*. I would also like to thank everyone else who helped me with the book – they know who they are.

First published in Great Britain in 1997 by Manchester United Books
an imprint of André Deutsch Ltd
106 Great Russell Street
London WC1B 3LJ
www.vci.co.uk

André Deutsch is a subsidiary of VCI plc

Published in association with
The Memorabilia Pack Company
16 Forth Street
Edinburgh EH1 3LH

Text © André Deutsch Ltd 1997

Printed and bound in Hong Kong by Dah Hua Printing Press Co. Ltd

A catalogue record for this book is available from the British Library

ISBN 0 233 99178 6

Designed by Don Macpherson

The Memorabilia Pack Company would like to thank the following for their assistance: Leslie Millman, Ray Adler, Dick Best, BBC Radio Ulster, Mark Wylie, Manchester United Football Club, Manchester Evening News, The Football Association and Wembley Stadium Limited.

CONTENTS

MATT BUSBY'S WAY

Bill Foulkes and Harry Gregg, two survivors of the Munich disaster, in action in August 1958.

Matt Busby and his wife Jean in their garden.

Matt Busby single-handedly shaped the creation of Manchester United as one of the world's greatest clubs. When he took control of United as manager in 1945, the club had an unexceptional history. The First Division title had been won twice, in 1907-8 and 1910-11, and the FA Cup just once, in 1909. It was a short roll of honour for a club that had been founded in 1878 as Newton Heath, becoming known as Manchester United in 1902.

Old Trafford, which had been opened in 1910, had been seriously damaged by German bombing during the Second World War; trees grew on the abandoned terraces. Since 1941 United had played their fixtures at Maine Road, the home of Manchester City. City were the dominant side in Manchester; United had drifted between the First and Second Divisions. Old Trafford was not the only football ground to have been bombed during the Second World War but Old Trafford and Manchester United would become matchless examples of postwar reconstruction.

In February 1945, when Busby took over, circumstances looked heavily weighted against him. But this 35-year-old had all that he required: a club with potential. Here he could put into practice the ideas he had accumulated as a canny right-half with Liverpool, Manchester City and Scotland. He was radical for those times in donning a tracksuit and joining his players on the pitch at training. He introduced new training methods whereby players practised frequently with the ball. Before then, managers had been besuited, aloof characters and footballers' training had consisted of hard running and little ballwork.

Busby was never a great tactician but he was a masterful judge of a player, both of an individual's abilities and their character. A reserved person, Busby weighed his words carefully and had the ability to motivate men. Three years after he had taken over, United won the FA Cup for the second time. They played exceptional attacking football in their 4-2 victory over Blackpool in the 1948 final, having overcome First Division opposition in all six rounds of the competition without requiring any replays. In Busby's first five seasons as manager, United finished second in the First Division four times and fourth once. Stars of those sides included left-back and captain Johnny Carey and the deft wingers Charlie Mitten and Jimmy Delaney.

Another of Busby's pioneering principles was a belief in a youth system. At Old Trafford young players would be given room in which to breathe and develop. As the 1950s progressed, Busby steadily introduced young players into his first-team. Players such as Roger Byrne provided early evidence that Busby's ideas were working; he was a mainstay of the team that won the League title in 1952 and became United captain at the age of 22 in February 1954. Busby's investment in youth was amply rewarded with further First Division titles in 1956 and 1957 and another FA Cup final appearance in 1957 when United lost, unluckily, 2-1 to Aston Villa.

The European Cup had been established in 1955 and had initially met with stubborn resistance from the English football authorties. Chelsea, the English League champions in 1955, were told not to compete in the new tournament and complied. When Manchester United won the English title in 1956, they were told that the ban would also apply to them. Busby, however, refused to be held back and United became the first English club to compete in Europe. In the words of the European Cup's founder, French sports journalist Gabriel Hanot: 'The new British champions Manchester United not only failed to commit the same mistake as their predecessors but entered the competition with a resolution and conviction which definitely consecrated the European Cup.'

In the 1956-57 European Cup, United reached the semi-finals, losing to eventual winners Real Madrid. Manchester United won the League again that 1956-57 season, enabling them to enter the European Cup for a second time. With several outstanding young players, most notably the 20-year-old Duncan Edwards, the team dubbed the 'Busby Babes' looked serious contenders for the trophy. Matt said of the Busby Babes tag: 'It wasn't a title I particularly liked, but it certainly stuck.'

In defeating Red Star Belgrade they reached the semi-finals. Tragically, on the journey home from Belgrade the plane carrying the United party crashed. The pilot had been attempting to take off after a stopover in Munich. Twenty-three passengers died on that day, 6 February 1958, including eight United players: Geoff Bent, Roger Byrne, Eddie Colman, Duncan Edwards, Mark Jones, David Pegg, Tommy Taylor and Bill Whelan.

Several other players were seriously injured and Busby, a devout Roman Catholic, was twice given the last rites as he fought for his life in hospital. When he discovered the extent of the casualties and deaths he almost lost the will to live. On his recovery and return to England, he was unwilling to return to football. His wife, Jean, persuaded him not to give up his life's work and to dedicate the rebuilding of the team to those who had died in the disaster, a team who, Hanot said, 'had given the European Cup its letters of nobility'.

A makeshift United side did reach the 1958 FA Cup Final, which they lost 2-0, to Bolton Wanderers. It was, however, certain that a thorough reconstruction of the team would have to be completed. It was going to be difficult for Busby to create a team for the 1960s that would match the one of the 1950s for style. He would do so. The team of the 1960s would surpass all previous United teams, playing football with enormous grace and elegance. It would be the living, breathing embodiment of all that Matt Busby held dear in football and in life.

Matt Busby leads his Manchester United team out for the 1957 FA Cup Final with Aston Villa. United lost the match 2-1. They were seriously hampered when goalkeeper Ray Wood had to leave the field after six minutes. Villa centre-forward Peter McParland's excessively heavy challenge had left him with a fractured cheek-bone.

THE SIXTIES

The 1960s saw a synthesis of style and substance in football that made it one of the most exciting decades in the history of the game. As with so much else in those years, a host of factors contributed to making football in the 1960s distinctively different to what came before and after.

The British game now had wider horizons. By 1960, European football had become established as an intrinsic part of the football scene. In that year, the European Cup had been competed for for the fifth time. Real Madrid had dominated the competition, playing football with a degree of style that had never been seen before. To British managers with an open mind about the game, such as Matt Busby at Manchester United, Real were an inspiration.

For the fans and the players, European football was a treat – a novelty and a rarity to be savoured. Only the elite from each country competed in European competition and the clash of styles between the representatives of the various countries made for fascinating entertainment. European matches were played in midweek, the green rectangle of the football pitch, the focus of so many lives, framed and thrown into sharp relief by the floodlights. That would have been impossible to do on a widespread basis in the previous decade. Floodlights had only become common during the late 1950s. At Old Trafford they had been introduced in 1957.

In Britain, managers such as Matt Busby, Bill Shankly at Liverpool and Jock Stein at Celtic attempted to build sides with the flexibility to compete successfully at both domestic and European level. The result of their endeavours would be teams that combined the craft of the continentals with the type of commitment and team spirit that had always been characteristic of Britain's football teams. Theirs would be the clubs that would epitomize the spirit of football in the 1960s.

It was a time when the English First Division was exactly that – the top division of the English Football League. Two points were awarded for a win and most sides went out looking for a win. It was difficult to do anything else: as the 1960s began the prevalent team formation was 2-3-5, consisting of two full-backs, three half-backs in the midfield and five forwards. It meant that teams were top-heavy in being weighted towards the search for goals but the fans were not complaining. It was not unusual for half-a-dozen goals or more to be scored in one game. On the continent, the Italians invented the ultra-defensive *catenaccio* system, employing a sweeper behind a four-man defence. It brought them European success but it remained alien to the British. By the late 1960s, however, English clubs' defences had tightened up; more defensive formations such as 4-3-3 and 4-4-2 having become standard.

Forwards were further aided in the 1960s by new lightweight equipment. Football boots improved in design throughout the decade, becoming more and more streamlined. Screw-in studs allowed players to easily adjust the grip on their boots to deal with different pitch surfaces. Nylon shorts and lighter shirts also helped to increase mobility. A new design of football, made, like the boots, of an improved standard of leather, was closer to being waterproof. That made accurate passing, for those with the ability to do so, easier; the ball did not retain water and grow heavier under wet conditions as the old bladders had done.

Team shirts were not yet adorned with the names of club sponsors. Indeed, it was unusual for the club crest to appear on team shirts during the 1960s outside of cup finals. Sponsorship, and its accompanying demands on players and managers, was almost non-existent. The media was less intrusive and managers and players were less in demand for 'quotes'. At the beginning of the 1960s, the sports pages of newspapers remained basic: dealing chiefly in team news, results and match reports. Reporters heard rumours of players' off-field activities but confined their reporting to events on the field.

The footballers of the 1960s remained, essentially, Saturday's men. A full fixture card was guaranteed every Saturday from late August to the end of April except when bad weather intervened. The FA Cup final took place on the first Saturday in May. Football would then close down until the start of the following season. However, with English clubs' increasing European commitments, the season was occasionally extended for certain clubs, such as Manchester United.

Televised football was a novelty. The BBC's Match of the Day was first broadcast in 1964 and matches were never moved from their original date to suit the purposes of television. Television reflected football; football did not reflect the demands of television. Only those matches that had been postponed, cup replays and European ties were played in midweek. Sundays were for perusing the results from the previous day. Live televised football was a rare treat, reserved for cup finals and key international matches.

Manchester United were Britain's best-supported club during the 1960s. Their fans, particularly those in the highly vocal Stretford End, played a strong supporting role in their team's victories.

Most spectators in the 1960s were on their feet throughout the match, regardless of how much excitement it generated. There were no all-seater stadiums in the whole of Britain. Most grounds had one main grandstand for the well-heeled but it would be dwarfed by the surrounding terraces. The opening of the new cantilevered stand at Old Trafford in 1965 gave Manchester United two facing stands but as in most aspects of football they were well ahead of the times. There were no fences penning the fans in; pitch invasions often took place at the end of matches.

Football remained largely the preserve of the working classes and season-ticket-holders made up only a small minority of crowds. Replica shirts were worn only for participating in football, not on the terraces or stands. Rosettes and simple bar scarves provided the colour on the terraces. A large number of adult fans at the beginning of the 1960s wore a collar-and-tie to matches. All-ticket matches were another rarity. At most matches, spectators arrived at the gate and handed over their few shillings. It meant that fans could decide right up to kick-off whether or not to go to a game. It also meant that those who made it a last-minute decision and turned up minutes before the start ran the risk of being locked out. United

An aerial view of Old Trafford in May 1966. Only the Scoreboard End remains uncovered, as it did throughout the 1960s.

were watched by massive crowds both at home and almost everywhere else. Players, as they have been throughout the history of football, were well paid. The abolition of the maximum wage of £20 a week in 1961 saw their wages increase steadily throughout the 1960s. Exceptional players such as George Best could earn more than their weekly wage through outside commitments.

In the FA Cup, a second replay would go to a neutral venue and in Europe no one had even thought of introducing a rule where away goals counted double when a match ended level on aggregate. Instead, a play-off would be arranged at a neutral venue. Penalty shoot-outs were non-existent.

For Manchester United, the 1960s began quietly with Matt Busby steadily and patiently rebuilding the team in the wake of the Munich disaster. The Old Trafford side remained massively popular worldwide as was shown in the warm receptions they met whenever they travelled to play a tie in European competition. They were received in style everywhere they went from Helsinki to Malta, often outstripping their local opponents in terms of popularity.

Football fans in the 1960s frequently applauded a skilful piece of play by an opposition player. Players often applauded each other off the park and in Matt Busby Manchester United had a manager who required high standards of play and sportsmanship from both himself and his players. He was 50 years old when the 1960s began and his paternal air helped keep things at Old Trafford steady during the rockiest times. In his football mind, however, he remained fresh and young, ready to adapt to the demands of a new era in football. He was ready to shape some magnificent moments for Manchester United in the 1960s.

SEASON 1959-60

The 1960s, a decade that would reveal a host of delights for Manchester United, began with the club in as mediocre a condition as they would ever be found under the management of Matt Busby. Their first match of the 1960s, away to Newcastle United on 2 January 1960, left them nine points behind First Division leaders Tottenham Hotspur and eight above the bottom club, Luton Town. They were a classic middle-of-the-table outfit both in their League position and their performances. A 7-3 defeat by Newcastle in front of a 57,000 crowd left them on the same points as the St James' Park side, a fellow 1950s giant that would spend much of the 1960s searching for the glories it had experienced in the previous decade. The major difference between United and their competitors, however, was that in Matt Busby they had a man who would not rest until he had rebuilt his team in a manner that would suit the special demands and challenges of the new decade.

Busby's side had signed off from the 1950s in a manner that suggested a continuing search for a renewed identity after the emotional aftershocks of the Munich disaster. The manager had stated that it would take five years for the club to be restored to full health after those heart-rending days and his side would, like a recovering patient, lurch unsteadily from match to match with varying results. Some days were better than others. Boxing Day 1959 had brought a 2-1 home defeat at the hands of Burnley; two days later, in the return fixture, United enjoyed a surprise 4-1 win. Outside-left Albert Scanlon, a survivor of Munich, looked particularly sharp. This was a victory over the side that would eventually take the 1959-60 First Division title.

The previous season had seen United rallying in the second half of the programme to finish 1958-59 as runners-up in the First Division. There was little chance of that in 1960, so the fans' attention focused on the FA Cup. After victories over Derby County and Liverpool in the third and fourth rounds, United were presented with a tough draw away to Sheffield Wednesday. Wednesday, a powerful, hard-working side, were fourth in the First Division. The tie was also tinged with sentiment: two years previously, amid highly emotional scenes, United had beaten Wednesday 3-0 in a

Matt Busby with Bobby Charlton. They enjoyed a successful partnership based on mutual respect.

fifth-round cup-tie that had been the club's first match after the 1958 Munich disaster. Two survivors of the air crash who had played that day, centre-half Bill Foulkes and goalkeeper Harry Gregg, were also in the side that took the field for another fifth-round tie between the sides. Albert Quixall, who had two years previously been in the defeated Wednesday side, lined up at inside-right against his old team. He had been signed by United for a British record transfer fee of £45,000 in September 1958 – £10,000 more than the previous record.

On 20 February 1960, a penalty-kick awarded to Wednesday on the hour settled a stirring, fast-flowing game that had lived up to all the pre-match expectations. United had all the creative ideas and flair. But a tendency to over-complicate their attacking movements made for some crazy patterns that eventually unravelled messily. While United had most of the play Wednesday's down-to-earth defending won on the day although the Yorkshire side were forced back upon all their resources in the closing stages. Two fine saves by Springett from United forwards Dennis Viollet and Bobby Charlton together with a goal-line clearance ensured that Wednesday hung on to their lead. Viollet ended that season as United's top scorer in the League with 32 goals, a record that has still to be beaten. Charlton had been a regular in the United team since making his debut in October 1956, aged 18.

Dennis Viollet, who set United's all-time League goalscoring record in the 1959-60 season, takes the field for a match at Arsenal.

In front of 66,000, Wednesday's crisp, attentive tackling and no-nonsense attacks had overpowered United. The goal itself had come from one of their characteristically simple attacks, a long pass into the United box pressurising half-back Maurice Setters into fouling Wednesday's Fantham to concede the decisive penalty. Setters had been Busby's first signing of the 1960s a month previously: for £30,000 from West Bromwich Albion, as a replacement for the injured Wilf McGuinness.

While Matt Busby was not above adopting some pragmatic measures when necessary he was never likely to follow the example of Wednesday and other clubs who used a similar style. He was dedicated to creating a style of football that fans could wallow in and was prepared to display patience in obtaining such a side rather than opt for short-term expediency. A basic form of football would, for a time, produce limited success in the English League but would count for little in the cultured company of Europe's best clubs.

After their exploits of the 1950s, United were still a massively popular club and shortly after that cup defeat it was announced that they would be sailing to North America in May 1960 for a ten-match tour of the USA and Canada, at the invitation of the North American Soccer League. They also possessed several internationals. In April 1960, Bobby Charlton, who had been given his first international cap at the age of 20 in 1958, was the outstanding England player in the 1-1 draw with Scotland at Hampden Park. He scored England's second-half equalizer from the penalty spot but also sent another penalty wide of goal despite taking two attempts to score from it. On the opposite side, Scotland's outstanding player was their 20-

year-old inside-forward Denis Law, then starring at Manchester City following his transfer from Huddersfield Town in March 1960.

As United played out their season, out of contention in League and Cup, there were still moments of enormous inspiration for their fans. On Easter Monday, West Ham United visited Old Trafford for a League match that highlighted United's strengths and weaknesses.

Bobby Charlton, playing in a free role, floating up and down the left wing, caused havoc for the Hammers. Johnny Giles, an immensely talented Dubliner aged just 19, performed a similar function on the right. Despite a 5-3 victory, United still appeared vulnerable to sides who were more methodical and better-organized, such as West Ham; regardless of United's wonderful flair, West Ham were unlucky not to get a draw. United had dominated from the start but had had to come from behind to get their victory, Alex Dawson connecting with Charlton's cross to make it 3-3 in the 49th minute before two further goals got them their win.

Charlton's talent had never been in doubt. Wilf McGuinness, later to manage United, joined the club on the same day as Charlton in 1953. Remembering playing alongside him for Manchester United's youth team and for England Schoolboys, McGuinness said of his contemporary: 'Even then you could see the grace and style that he had. The talent and the smoothness was there. He was like a thoroughbred, a racehorse, he moved so majestically at times. He oozed class. He was like a ballet dancer in many ways, graceful with power.'

Although Charlton had looked comfortable on the wing in that match against West Ham it would still be some time before he would move into the central attacking midfield role with which he would become England's most famous and most inspirational player of the 1960s. In 1961, he was still playing on the wing but looking for a bit more of the action. 'Inside-forwards have a much harder time than we wingers,' he wrote in the *International Football Book No. 3*. 'In spite of that, I would still eventually find more satisfaction in a return to an inside-forward position, should "The Boss" [as all of his players automatically referred to Busby] come to think me sufficiently mature ... inside, one is more in the game for longer spells. It gives more satisfaction. You are less likely to let your mind wander, and lose that all-important concentration.'

In conclusion, he added: 'To watch good players is the most rewarding thing in football. You may forget particular matches, but you can never forget them. They are the real wealth in football, and I can never tire of seeing top-class players create something within a game. What's more, they obviously enjoy it! That's why I crave the experience that will enable me to make the most of what I've got. So that one day I too can create something, consistently and well. Something that might be remembered.'

Few footballers have conjured up a more prescient vision of their future years. Over the next decade, with assistance from some distinguished colleagues, Bobby Charlton would make those words come true almost to the letter. As a clear outline of the career ahead of him they could hardly be bettered.

Cassius Clay claims boxing gold for the USA at the 1960 Olympics in Rome. On returning home, Clay was so disgusted at still finding endemic racism rampant that he threw his Olympic medal into a river. Clay, who later changed his name to Mohammed Ali, was a sporting hero to millions in the 1960s. Among them was George Best, who was completely overawed when he got the chance to meet the boxer.

SEASON
1960-61

United made a surprisingly bad start to the first full season of the 1960s. In their League campaign they lost seven goals in two opening defeats. They still drew a crowd of 51,818 to Old Trafford on the final day of August when, in their third match of the season, they enjoyed a 4-0 win over an improving Everton side. An opportunity to re-establish themselves as credible championship challengers quickly arrived with a visit to Tottenham three days later. Spurs were widely regarded as the finest side in the country. They had been the popular choice for champions the previous season before being pipped by Burnley. The Londoners had acquired maximum points from their first three League games and one of the perennial classic matches in the English football calendar fully lived up to its reputation for excellence.

United had had a good record at White Hart Lane in the previous few seasons but in the opening half-hour of this match they were simply played off the park by what was fast becoming one of the greatest of all English club sides as Spurs sped to a 4-1 win.

Frank Haydock and Jimmy Nicholson, two of United's three half-backs in the 2-3-5 formation that was commonplace at the time, were both teenagers and often found proceedings passing them by because of the speed and imagination of Spurs' play. Charlton and Viollet were among the few United players who looked capable of adapting to the ultra-modern passing game being played by their opponents. The Munich hangover remained naggingly present: United were still in the position of having to field youngsters in the first-team before Busby would ideally have liked to do so.

The match at White Hart Lane underlined how far United had to go to achieve parity with the best English sides before Busby could turn his eyes towards Europe once again. That was the arena in which he knew the reputations of the great sides of the 1960s would be forged.

The remaining five fixtures in September brought United just three points and by the time of their meeting with Bolton Wanderers at Burnden Park on 1 October they were third bottom of the First Division and without an away point in the League. The fixture aroused most interest through the return to their team of Bolton's centre-forward Nat Lofthouse, who had been missing for 18 months through injury. Lofthouse had also been involved in one of the most controversial moments in English football history when he barged United goalkeeper Harry Gregg over the line in the 1958 Cup final for Bolton's second goal in their 2-0 win over United. While Lofthouse, one of England's most potent players of the 1950s, was coming to the end of his career, a man who would be one of his country's stars of the 1960s was making his senior debut for United – Nobby Stiles. A hard-fought 1-1 draw moved United up one place in the First Division.

Just under a fortnight later, United's faithful had an opportunity to take a mini-holiday from watching their favourites struggle in the English League when United faced Real Madrid in a friendly match at Old Trafford. Five months earlier, Real had won their fifth consecutive European Cup in one of the most memorable matches ever seen in world football; the 7-3 defeat of Eintracht Frankfurt at Hampden Park, Glasgow.

It was the third friendly match between United and Real thanks to a generous offer by Real president Santiago Bernabeu. In an act of compassion shortly after the Munich disaster, he had, on meeting Matt Busby in Madrid, told the United manager that he would waive Real's usual hefty fee for friendlies and that the Old Trafford club should pay only what it could afford to the great Spanish club for providing the opposition in such matches.

Alfredo Di Stefano, the Argentinian who was Busby's favourite player, led Real with some panache on that October evening. As Busby had always anticipated, the high standard of the opposition raised United's own game. A crowd of 51,000 witnessed United's best performance of the season up to that point. Along with Real's sophisticated passing game, another example of futuristic football was provided when Real, by agreement with United, used four substitutes. This was five years before substitutes were allowed in League matches in England. Prominent figures in the English game, such as Sir Stanley Rous, chairman of the FA, fulminated publicly and at length against the very idea of substitutes.

Charlton, Stiles, Nicholson, inside-left Mark Pearson and Setters were all particularly uplifted by the occasion. A subtle header from Pearson and a 20-yard shot from Nicholson were United's replies to goals by Di Stefano, Vidal and Rial. All five goals were magnificent and the crowd was enthused by the grand nature of the occasion. It was Real's third win in this series of friendlies with United and it served as a tempting taste of what great European nights might bring. At times, United had shown themselves capable of competing with Europe's best on equal terms although Real's greats had approached this game in a relaxed, friendly fashion.

Busby had an almost evangelical zeal for European competitition. Writing in the *International Football Book No. 3* in 1961 he stated: 'Football followers in Britain have never taken sufficient interest in the game abroad. Even though the situation has improved during the past five years or so, we still tend to hold ourselves a little aloof from foreign footballing affairs.

'It could be that the public need educating. After all, people cannot be entirely blamed for ignoring the great players and teams in Europe and South America, when British newspapers and periodicals consistently fail to supply news from abroad...

Harry Gregg uses an upright for support as he tips the ball over the bar in United's 4-4 draw at Fulham in December 1960.

13

'But at least we are now reasonably conversant with the affairs of Di Stefano, Puskas, Kopa, Yashin and the other big names. We also take an interest in important results concerning teams like Barcelona, Real Madrid, Juventus and Rheims.'

Much of that education was down to the progressive Busby and there was no mistaking where his long-term ambitions for Manchester United lay. He continued: 'The European Cup, a wonderful competition, has done much for football – one of its not-so-obvious advantages being the way it has introduced Continental teams and players to the British public. This must surely have broadened the outlook of football followers in Manchester, Wolverhampton, Burnley, Glasgow, Edinburgh and Belfast.'

Few football managers, then and now, could or would wish to express themselves so expansively. Busby's relish for testing his teams against the best available served as a spur as he pieced together another team that might allow him to experience competitive European football once again.

The exotic nature of the evening with Real was emphasised by United's continuing struggles in the League during the final three months of 1960. But a successful series of Christmas fixtures, including a 6-0 win over Chelsea on Boxing Day, moved them into tenth position in the First Division. They were well off the pace in the title race but their accelerating progress made them look up-to-speed for a run in the FA Cup.

The year ended with a derby between United and City, both of whom had run into good form. A 5-1 win in front of 61,000 eased United into eighth position. Alex Dawson attained the first hat-trick in a Manchester derby since Joe Spence had scored three for United in October 1921; Bobby Charlton got the other two. In early March, goals from Dawson, Charlton and Pearson at Maine Road in a 3-1 win against City ensured that United were the top team in Manchester.

A 3-0 home win over Middlesbrough in the FA Cup brought United another tie with Sheffield Wednesday, this time at Hillsborough. After a 1-1 draw, 65,000 attended Old Trafford for the replay. Again, Wednesday's cold pragmatism was to win the day although with the score at 1-1 two vital slips by United goalkeeper Ronnie Briggs, called into the team as a replacement for the injured Gregg, helped Wednesday move into the fifth round. A Finney shot slipped through Briggs' hands to make it 2-1 then a hesitant Briggs let Ellis head Wednesday's third. Briggs was then unlucky when he got to an Ellis shot but saw the loose ball squirm over the line to make it 4-1 to Wednesday at half-time. Wednesday ended up 7-2 winners.

There was, however, an encouraging improvement in United's play during the second half of the season and they finished seventh in the First Division, well clear of the relegation trouble that had been threatening them before Christmas. And one particular match in mid-January – the return with champions-elect Spurs at Old Trafford – had fired the hopes of United fans.

United set about their celebrated opponents with gusto, keeping Spurs at bay even when goalkeeper Gregg received a serious shoulder injury during a goalmouth scramble shortly before half-time. (That would keep Gregg out of the FA Cup match with Sheffield Wednesday a fortnight later.) Gregg passed his green jersey to Dawson who replaced him in goal.

In those pre-substitute days, any injured player who could still remain upright, however badly handicapped in terms of being able to move about, would be kept on the pitch, for nuisance value if nothing else. So in the second half against Spurs, Gregg, although unfit to remain in goal, hobbled about at centre-forward with his shoulder strapped up. By then, United were defending a 1-0 lead that had been secured in the 14th minute. A determined run by Pearson set up Quixall, whose shot was parried by

Johnny Giles, a clever midfielder who turned 20 in November 1960, was one of the most promising prospects at Old Trafford during the 1960-61 season.

Spurs goalkeeper Brown. Stiles, following up, slipped the ball into the net.

In that match with Spurs, United showed that, when they applied their minds to it, they could be creative and calculating in equal measures. They still attacked with flair but they also tackled hard and chased back whenever they lost possession. Pearson, Quixall and Charlton were at their mercurial best. Their classical touches lit up the play but the decisive goal was one of the most bizarre ever seen at Old Trafford. Gregg, still up with the forwards, backheeled the ball in a fashion that would not have disgraced a Di Stefano or a Puskas. It dropped neatly into the path of Pearson, who sent the ball past Brown and consigned Spurs to one of only seven defeats in cup and League during the 1960-61 season.

The White Hart Lane side would go on to become the first this century to win the double. United had shown that, on their day, they could live with them. Such glimpses of greatness helped nurture great expectations among the United fans. A return to the days of glory appeared to be within tantalizing touching distance.

SEASON 1961-62

The 1961-62 season saw United continuing to evolve slowly into more credible challengers for England's honours. The side's inconsistency, however, saw them remain more of a cup side than one yet able to weather the vicissitudes of an eight-month campaign to bring home the championship.

During the summer, Busby had paid Arsenal £35,000 for their centre-forward David Herd whose father Alec had played alongside Busby for Manchester City during the 1930s. The purchase of Herd signalled the end of Alex Dawson's Old Trafford career and soon after he joined Preston North End. Herd had a quiet debut in the first game of the season, away to West Ham. It was Nobby Stiles who scored United's opening goal from close to the penalty spot. Viollet had patiently held on to the ball then floated it over the West Ham defence to the running Stiles. Viollet and Mark Pearson were particularly inventive and late in the match a Viollet shot rebounded off the angle of bar and post. The Reds returned to Old Trafford with a 1-1 draw.

United had started the season in fluid fashion and a 3-2 win over Chelsea in their next match appeared to consolidate United's pre-season position among the favourites to take the championship. That was followed by a 6-1 victory over Blackburn in which Herd scored his first two goals for the club, the start of an impressive tally of goals that he would quietly accumulate for United during the 1960s. United's sixth goal in that match

David Herd was 28 when Matt Busby signed him from Arsenal in the summer of 1961. He would give United seven years of steady goalscoring and goalmaking service.

was a 40-yard shot from Setters and as well as occasionally contributing to the attack he and his fellow half-back Stiles appeared to be ensuring that United were now, finally, sturdy and resilient at the back. Charlton continued to provide United's most extravagant touches from his position on the left wing.

United remained among the leading clubs until a disastrous two-month run that began on the final day of September with a 2-0 defeat at Wolves. By the time they met Burnley at Old Trafford at the end of November they had taken just two points from their previous eight matches and were uncomfortably close to the relegation places. Herd opened the scoring with a well-taken header from Bradley's cross but after a bright opening 20 minutes United crumbled. Burnley were top of the First Division and the gap between them and United was heavily emphasized as the away side powered on to a 4-1 win. United's slight inside-forwards Giles and Quixall simply bounced off Burnley's tough defensive minders.

That match at Burnley was followed by a 5-1 defeat at Everton, then two home matches that brought a win over Fulham and a defeat from West Ham. On Boxing Day, United clawed back a bit more self-respect. On an Old Trafford surface that resembled a much-toyed-with Christmas pudding, they defeated Nottingham Forest 6-3 in a match in which they showed sporadic touches of great style despite having started the game in second-bottom position in the First Division. Watched by 31,366 – a poor attendance for United that reflected their position – half-back 'Nobby' Lawton scored a fine hat-trick; Brennan, Herd and Charlton got the other goals.

Yet again, United sought solace in the FA Cup. For their third-round tie at home to Bolton Wanderers Giles had recovered from a cold; Charlton had not. Despite missing their most inspirational player, luck was on United's side. Trailing 1-0 with seven minutes of the match remaining, Herd equalized despite having looked slightly offside. Wanderers' players, who had protested long and hard to referee Mr Howell from Birmingham, were still feeling aggrieved when United got a 90th-minute winner, a long-range shot from Nicholson kissing the inside of the post on its way into the net. The only worry for the soon-departing 42,000 crowd was whether United had used up all their cup luck in the one game.

There were 12,000 more at the next tie, at home to Arsenal. This was another of those early-1960s occasions on which it appeared as though United had found a potent blend of flair players and masterful defenders. On an evening of torrential rain, United appeared to have been refreshed rather than impeded by the elements. Centre-half Foulkes in particular was outstanding while Stiles, having been moved into the forward line to compensate for the injured Herd, displayed inventiveness and some assured touches.

The only goal of the match arrived after 28 minutes. Winger Phil Chisnall floated a corner into the penalty area where Setters found a gap to head the ball firmly into the net. That set up a third cup meeting in successive years between United and Sheffield Wednesday. A 0-0 draw at Old Trafford saw United run out of ideas before half-time. That took them to Hillsborough for the replay with the bonus that Foulkes, missing from the Old Trafford encounter, was back in place at the centre of the defence. This time, United were composed and carefully constructive while waves of Wednesday attacks crashed off the Old

A fee of £29,500 made Noel Cantwell the most expensive full-back in Britain when Matt Busby signed him from West Ham in 1960. The experienced Irish international became club captain.

Trafford side's strong defensive barriers. With 65,000 watching, United took the lead in eight minutes when a mesmerizing five-man move ended with Giles playing a natty one-two with Herd before beating Wednesday goalkeeper Springett. With 73 minutes gone, Charlton took a pass from Stiles, eluded the flailing boots of two defenders and slammed a right-footed shot past Springett to send United into a quarter-final with Liverpool or Preston. Those two sides were scheduled to meet each other in a second replay the following week at the neutral venue of Old Trafford.

Preston it was, and at Deepdale Alex Dawson lined up at centre-forward against his former United mates. United were without Herd, Quixall and Stiles while defender Noel Cantwell, making his first appearance since November, was a makeshift centre-forward. United were lucky to get a 0-0 draw and a replay but four days later 63,000 turned up at Old

One of United's most colourful players of the early 1960s was Albert Quixall who cost £45,000, by far a new British record transfer fee, when signed from Sheffield Wednesday in 1958.

Trafford looking to cheer their heroes into the semi-final. Their expectations of victory were heightened by the return of Herd, Quixall and Stiles and, as so often, it was Bobby Charlton who sparked off the victory. After 27 minutes he left several defenders trailing before slipping in the opener. Ten minutes later, he fed Herd who applied a stylish finish for United's decisive second goal. That victory took the Reds back to Hillsborough for the FA Cup semi-final. There they faced Tottenham who had reached the semi-finals of the European as well as the domestic cup.

It was United's most important match of the 1960s up to that point but on the day they were brushed aside by Spurs with the ease of a Jaguar overtaking a Mini on its way to a more important destination. United were not helped by several players having an off-day although goalkeeper David Gaskell was not one of them. Only Charlton and Quixall were up to scratch in attack while Foulkes and Cantwell were their reliable selves in defence.

After just four minutes Jimmy Greaves opened the scoring for Spurs and Jones added a second goal 20 minutes later. Greaves also had Stiles make a goal-line clearance although Charlton did go close for United. With eight minutes remaining, a scintillating run and shot from Charlton span, on the rebound from the Spurs goalkeeper, to Herd, who scored. Three minutes from time, however, Spurs' Medwin delivered the killer blow.

A week later, United had recovered sufficiently to register a 5-0 home win over Ipswich Town (managed by Alf Ramsey), who were to go on to win the First Division title that season. Pick of the goals was a 25-yarder from Quixall, (one of three goals for him in that match) the others being scored by Stiles and Setters. In the final reckoning, United had, as so often, won a battle with little indication of being prepared for any long drawn out wars. They finished the season 14 places below Ipswich. It was the club's lowest First Division placing, up to that point, in the 17 years Busby had been in charge at Old Trafford. It appeared as though things could only get better the following season. They did, but in a manner few expected. It was to prove one of the most dramatic and significant seasons in United's history.

SEASON 1962-63

If a player could have been specially designed for Manchester United, the specification would have produced an individual close in character to Denis Law. He scored with style, making it look deceptively easy to the point where he seemed to put more effort into his strutting post-goal celebrations than into his finishing. Lean and quick, he appeared to create new geometric angles as he twisted and turned with equal effectiveness in the air and on the ground to direct the ball towards the target.

Matt Busby had been aware of Law's skills even before his debut as a 16-year-old under Bill Shankly at Second Division Huddersfield. Busby had a vivid memory of the first time he had seen the player: 'When we were losing 2-0 at half-time in a youth match at Heckmondwike, I wondered who was taking us apart. Then I realized it was a little will-o'-the-wisp called Law, who had also scored both goals. I knew then that Huddersfield had found someone more than a bit special.'

Law, on deciding to leave Huddersfield shortly after Shankly had taken over as manager of Liverpool in December 1959, would have followed his mentor to Anfield. But he did not fancy moving from one Second Division club to another. Instead, he had gone to Manchester City for £53,000 in March 1960 and became the first £100,000 player when he moved from there to Torino in the summer of 1961. Unhappy with the strictly regimented ways of football in Italy he became available for transfer less than a year later. After more than two months of complicated legal wrangling and negotiations between Manchester United and Torino, Law finally signed for Busby in July 1962, for a British record fee of £115,000.

Law, who would go on to become Scotland's greatest-ever goalscorer, had become the youngest player to represent his country in the twentieth century when given his international debut at the age of 18. The man who had picked him was the then acting Scotland boss Matt Busby, who was combining the duties of Scotland and Manchester United manager. Law had rewarded Busby by scoring in that match against Wales in 1958.

'It was the swinging sixties and everyone was having a great time, weren't they?' remembered Law. 'It was no different in Manchester. The atmosphere of life was so different then, it was like a ten-year party. At Old Trafford there were great players and it was good to be part of Matt's set-up. I'd played under Matt for Scotland and I knew the man so I hoped it would be the beginning of something good.'

It wouldn't have been like Denis to have a quiet debut and he didn't. There was pandemonium at Old Trafford after seven minutes of his first game for the club when Giles' clever chip was subtly directed into the corner of the West Brom net by an almost imperceptible flick of Law's head. That put United two up; they had gone ahead when Herd scored after 90 seconds. A quick free-kick from Stiles picked out the centre-forward just inside the West Brom half and he flew towards goal, hardly breaking stride as he smacked in the opener. Few watching would have believed it, but those opening ten minutes could be classified as the highest peak of United's League season. The afternoon ended in disappointment as United conceded two late goals and found themselves being slow-handclapped by their fans in the closing stages – an ominous sign so early in the season.

There were 70,000 at Goodison Park for United's next match, a 3-1 defeat by Everton, and in the return at Old Trafford a week later, in front of a capacity crowd of 64,000 Jimmy Gabriel kept the shackles on Law. Everton got another victory thanks to a penalty ten minutes from time. In between, United had managed a victory over Arsenal, but between then and Christmas their League form was indifferent – they took 19 points from 19 games – and it was to worsen during the second half of the season. On Boxing Day they got a welcome 1-0 win at Fulham but a severe winter meant that that was their last fixture for nearly two months. Two League draws on their return to action in February did little to cheer United's fans and, once again, they looked to the cup as the season's salvation.

Pat Crerand's precision passing was a welcome addition to United's repertoire when he signed from Celtic in 1963.

Busby had not been idle during the enforced break. He had made one of his key signings of the 1960s in obtaining Pat Crerand, a pass-master of a right-half, from Celtic for £56,000. Crerand had been unsettled at Celtic Park for some time. Things had come to a head on New Year's Day 1963 when he had a stand-up argument in the dressing-room with Celtic assistant manager Sean Fallon at half-time in a match with Rangers. It was an indication of the fiery competitiveness he would bring to England. Crerand would be the inspiration behind many future victories. He signed on 6 February – the fifth anniversary of the Munich disaster.

On 4 March, a two-month-postponed third-round FA Cup tie against Huddersfield in front of 47,703 at Old Trafford gave United a much-needed boost. After three minutes Law carved his way deep into the Huddersfield half and touched the ball to Quixall who edged it into the net.

Eight minutes later, Herd cleverly found Setters who gave Law the opportunity to sprint away and make it 2-0 by hammering the ball high into goal. With 20 minutes gone, Charlton's sleek pass to Giles resulted in a shot from the Irishman that hit the foot of a post and rolled into the net. Midway through the first-half, Law made it four after cheekily pretending to miskick the ball. Charlton forced two fine saves from goalkeeper Ray Wood, and had a penalty turned down before half-time. A host of chances were missed by United in the second half. But two minutes from time, Charlton's floated ball found Law's head for 5-0. When United were on song they could hit all the right notes.

With fixtures to catch up on, United then went on to a fast-track route in the cup. Just a week after the Huddersfield tie, they met Aston Villa in the fourth round at Old Trafford. Villa were the more dynamic side and had most of the pressure. Boots were flying all night in a hard but fair encounter but in the 36th minute United got in the only blow that really mattered. Giles, Charlton and Law bamboozled the Villa defence, leaving Quixall to prod the ball under Villa goalkeeper Sidebottom for what would be the only goal of the game. A crowd of 52,000 saw United's strong-minded defence hold on for the rest of the match.

Then, only five days after the Villa tie, United faced Chelsea at home in the fifth round. In 17 minutes, Quixall chased Setters' long ball to the goal-line before cutting it back for Law to open the scoring. A minute after half-time a soft shot from Quixall beat Bonetti for the second. Chelsea played the prettier football and pulled a goal back late in the match but northern grit won the day.

At Coventry in the cup quarter-final just a fortnight later, United played their fourth cup tie in March. At Highfield Road, United's players were greeted by a far-from-tasty playing surface that consisted of a sand and sawdust topping over a thick layer of mud. It was not a day for niceties. Third-Division side Coventry had gone 23 matches without defeat. Ken Dodd and community singing were among the pleasures on display before the kick-off.

A furious start by Coventry gave them a fifth-minute lead but United equalized in the 27th minute. Setters' throw-in was moved on by Quixall to Law who found Charlton. The England man did the honours with a right-foot shot. Two further stunning goals – one from Quixall and one from Charlton – eased United into the semis.

Despite working like clockwork in the cup, United's League form remained amazingly unpredictable. Often, they would display their skills without the requisite teamwork; less often, the teamwork would be present without the flair. Rarely did the twain meet. An example of that came when United visited Leicester in mid-April 1963. Law had scored a hat-trick and Crerand had been spraying passes around the pitch all afternoon. Yet United had lost 4-3. It was desperately disappointing that such performances should not be rewarded with even a point, never mind a win.

Against Wolves a week later, the forwards and half-backs played creatively but were lax in carrying out their defensive duties. They also tended to be rather cavalier in spurning the chances they courted so cleverly. Wolves had been in the running for the championship but two magnificent goals, from Herd and Law, gave United a 2-1 win. Both goals came on the end of stylish, sophisticated moves but both also required the scorer to embellish the movement; Herd's powerful header and Law's smart shot on the run brooking no argument. In contrast, a series of much easier chances were missed by United. Even at the end, after Gaskell had pulled off a series of saves, Law scooped the ball over the bar when the simplest of touches appeared to be all that would be required for a third goal.

On 27 April, 68,312 people paid £28,499, seven shillings and sixpence – record receipts for Villa Park – to see the FA Cup semi-final between Manchester United, fourth bottom of the First Division, and Southampton, seventh bottom of the Second. The overbearing statistics of their League positions pointed to a dour relegation-type struggle and that was how it turned out.

Quixall and Brennan were unfit and were replaced for the semi-final by Giles and Cantwell. Giles, playing on the right flank, teamed up with Stiles at inside-right and Crerand at right-half. That talented trio carefully destabilized Southampton's back line on a day when defences dominated. In 11 minutes Giles hit the Southampton post after a long pass from Herd had set him free. And centre-forward Herd was the creator again 11 minutes later when he sought Law's head with a cross. Denis mistimed his jump but made a quick recovery to prod the ball over the line after he and it had fallen to earth simultaneously. It was all that was required for United to reserve their place at Wembley.

United were in their fourth final since the Second World War. Their opponents would be Leicester City who had defeated Liverpool 1-0 at Hillsborough in the other semi-final.

May began with 32,000 witnessing a home defeat to Sheffield Wednesday. In the opening stages United swirled all over their opponents' half but Wednesday were the more clinical of the two sides and went 3-0 up before Setters climbed high to head Crerand's cross into goal. It was another dysfunctional League performance from United although Stiles and Setters stood out because of their purposefulness and Law and Charlton showed occasional flashes of inspiration.

The harsh winter had resulted in the season being extended and the Cup final, originally scheduled for 4 May, was moved to 25 May. On the day when United's fans had expected to be partying in London, their team's lassitude in the League meant they were involved in the serious business of avoiding relegation. But on that day a 1-0 win over Burnley provided them with some peace of mind. Law had eased United's troubles with a magnificent header from Quixall's cross, the 25th of 30 goals he would score for United that season. 'Denis was in the same class as Di Stefano because he could do everything; organize a side and score goals. He was a man's man who could look after himself on the field and was a good professional off it,' said Harry Gregg.

Even a 3-2 home defeat to Arsenal two days later had its encouraging aspects, being notable for United's battling team spirit. Two well-taken goals by Law kept United in contention for the points right to the end and the Scot was unlucky to have a possible third ruled out for offside.

Luck was firmly on United's side when, after a defeat by Birmingham, they went to Maine Road for a match that seemed likely to decide which of the two relegation-threatened Manchester clubs would be likely to drop into the Second Division.

City took an eighth-minute lead through Harley and, in front of 52,484 spectators, Charlton, Law and Herd struggled throughout to find a way past the City defenders. City were unfortunate to have a goal disallowed before half-time and Gaskell saved well from Harley before United got a penalty six minutes from time. Law intercepted an inaccurate long-range pass-back from Wagstaffe and as he and City goalkeeper Dowd tussled for the ball Dowd appeared to grab Law's ankles. Quixall stepped up to take the penalty that instantaneously wiped out all of City's previous good work and left United closer to an escape from the drop. That 1-1 draw left City in second-bottom place on 31 points while United had a point more and were three places higher. They also had two games remaining while City had just one. City were duly relegated after a 6-1 defeat at West Ham. The next Manchester derby would not take place until September 1966.

From that point, the 1960s would be all about fun on the Old Trafford side of Manchester as United's confidence grew and grew.

United had finished 19th in the League and had had the luck of the draw on their Wembley way. United's team was, by far, the most expensive line-up ever to take the field for a Wembley final; six of their players had cost a total of over £300,000. It was their opponents, Leicester City, however, who were strong favourites to win. They were a side who relied on defending in numbers and hitting hard on the break.

During the League season, Leicester had been in contention for the First Division title but, with the slate wiped clean for the English season's crowning glory, United proved to be the team in command, making this one of the most one-sided finals Wembley had ever seen. United's display on that day belied many of their stuttering performances that season. Rid of any signs of a stammer, they expressed themselves fluently and expansively. The team's talented individuals clubbed together for a joint donation of effort that secured the trophy. Even in the midst of such impressive collectivism, Crerand and Law were a cut above the rest.

THE FOOTBALL ASSOCIATION CHALLENGE CUP COMPETITION

THE FOOTBALL ASSOCIATION   CENTENARY YEAR

1863   1963

FINAL TIE

LEICESTER CITY

v

MANCHESTER UNITED

OFFICIAL PROGRAMME   ONE SHILLING

WEMBLEY

EMPIRE STADIUM

SATURDAY, MAY 25th   Kick-off 3 p.m.

A nervy start had seen Gaskell, who alternated in goal with Gregg during that period, let slip the ball, an indiscretion that was corrected by Foulkes' speedy clearance. That was shortly after Giles had poked a shot past the Leicester post.

On the half hour, an expansive United move ended with Charlton's shot stretching Banks in the Leicester goal. Crerand intercepted the goalkeeper's throw-out, beat two defenders, raced into the penalty area and found Law twelve yards out. First controlling the ball with his left foot, he then swivelled through 180 degrees for a low, right-footed shot that gave Banks no chance to excel again. Shortly before half-time, Law's deception drew Banks from his goal. Only a desperate combination of effort from Norman and McLintock on the Leicester goal-line prevented United enjoying a 2-0 lead with their half-time tea.

Twelve minutes after the break, Gaskell threw the ball out to Giles who swiftly moved it, crossfield, on to Charlton. Banks could not hold on to the forward's resultant shot and Herd made it 2-0. A brief flurry of Leicester pressure brought them a goal with 10 minutes remaining. That sparked a glorious header from Law that came back off an upright into Banks' arms. The ever-emotional Law sank to his knees in desperation at his bad luck and buried his face in the Wembley turf. But the decisive goal was close at hand. Five minutes from time, Banks dropped Giles' cross and Herd was on the spot to finish the scoring at 3-1 to United.

On the day after the final, United arrived at Manchester's Central Station where they passed under a speedily-erected red-and-white triumphal arch. The streets were lined by 300,000 Mancunians who greeted the United party with an outpouring of emotion that had been bottled up since the Munich disaster. It took the victory bus about 45 minutes to travel the mile from the station to Albert Square and 400

United's Bill Foulkes helps out goalkeeper David Gaskell during the 1963 FA Cup Final between Manchester United and Leicester City (below) while Noel Cantwell (bottom) aids the attack. David Herd (below left) scores United's third in the 3-1 win.

people were treated for injuries in the inevitable crushing.

It was the most exceptional reception any victorious Manchester side had seen up to that point. On greeting the United party at Albert Square, the Lord Mayor, Alderman RC Rodgers, said: 'It was the finest game ever played at Wembley.'

SATURDAY

Evening News

Evening Chronicle **Chronicle & News** PRICE 3d.

WEMBLEY HOMECOMING SOUVENIR

No. 41

UNITED'S FINEST HOUR!

Captain Cantwell leads the cup-winning celebrations.

Team captain Noel Cantwell told the crowd that their reception that Sunday evening had made it the complete football weekend: 'It is absolutely fabulous. We knew there would be a crowd to greet us, but we never expected anything like this.'

Busby's immense patience over the preceding five years had been rewarded with the type of performance that would win United trophies and fans throughout the world. 'When I went into management,' Busby was to say, 'I did so with the idea that I should treat players in the way I would have wanted to be treated myself. That is probably one of the reasons I have had a bit of success.' Busby had always had belief in his players. That cup win would give them renewed belief in themselves.

SEASON 1963-64

A belief in the renewed vitality of Manchester United remained with the fans throughout the summer, as was shown by the attendance of 62,965 that greeted the players as they stepped on to the pitch for the first Old Trafford Saturday fixture of the 1963-64 season. United had started well, with a 3-3 draw away to Sheffield Wednesday and a 2-0 home win over Ipswich Town the following midweek. This match, though, looked sure to give them a thorough test: their opponents were Everton, the current champions. Thousands of fans were locked out but kept their ears to the ground, milling around outside Old Trafford in an attempt to gauge the progress of the match by listening to the roars of the crowd inside.

Two weeks previously, in the Charity Shield match at Goodison Park, the champions had made United look amateurish in a 4-0 defeat. In the League match, Tony Dunne, United's left-back, deflected a Vernon shot past Gregg to put United 1-0 behind after eight minutes. From then on, the fans outside would hear the sound of Everton being well-beaten as United swept on to a 5-1 victory.

The key to this Old Trafford triumph had been intricate teamwork allied to the players' profound belief in their abilities. After scoring United's fourth goal, Law had gesticulated to the fans, asking them whether they were satisfied with four goals. He made sure they were even happier, whatever their feelings, by making it 5-1 after 80 minutes. Even then, Pat Crerand missed a straightforward chance to make it six. After United's fifth goal, Bobby Charlton celebrated exuberantly, leaping high in the air, arms raised and heels almost level with his waist. Such unrestrained celebrations reflected how good feeling was coursing unstoppably through the team.

Three days on, at Portman Road, United took just four minutes to find the right combination to unlock the Ipswich defence; David Sadler, a 17-year-old who had been drafted into the side at the start of the season at centre-forward in place of David Herd, darted in for the opening goal. United's attack was operating with the swiftness and effectiveness of an electric-light switch: there was no wastage of energy in their attacking movements. At the back, Gregg, who saved a penalty when United were 3-1 ahead, and the centre-half Foulkes were establishing a brick-hard solidity in United's defence.

Again Law, who acknowledged the crowd with a regal wave after scoring United's seventh goal a few minutes from the end of a 7-2 win, was at the hub of most of the attacking excitement. Inside-right Phil Chisnall, who had also been one of the top men against Everton, was equally eye-catching in this game, not least for chipping in United's sixth goal.

Sean Connery made his first appearance as James Bond in the 1962 movie Dr No. *The Bond character as played by Connery would become synonymous with the 1960s. However, Connery almost came to prominence as a 1950s footballer. In 1953, at the age of 23, Connery, while working in the chorus of* South Pacific *in Manchester, received a phone call from Matt Busby asking him to join Manchester United. 'It was a great temptation,' said Connery. But he decided to concentrate on acting as a career.*

Johnny Giles, frustrated at being dropped for the Sheffield Wednesday match, had asked for a transfer and was quickly moved on to Second Division Leeds United for £35,000.

Those fine opening results meant that United topped the First Division table as they travelled to Birmingham City on the first Saturday in September. After five minutes of the match, Chisnall, with the help of a slight deflection, scored his fourth goal in three games and United looked on course for another victory. But Law, Charlton and winger Ian Moir were blanked by fine goalkeeping from Withers on three notable occasions before ex-Manchester City centre-forward Harley equalized with 15 minutes remaining.

Although United again displayed excellent all-round unity, this game had shown that they could still be put off their stride by less skilful but more determined opponents snapping at their heels.

NOBBY STILES
MANCHESTER UNITED

LEFT HALF

Still on top of the League, United were back on track the following midweek at home to Blackpool. Charlton, Sadler, Chisnall and Crerand were in potent form but they were high-quality bit-part players in comparison with Law. He was the star soloist, being denied the bouquet of goals his performance deserved only by the excellence of Waiters in the Blackpool goal.

A minute before half-time, Law played a high-speed one-two with Chisnall before sending the ball past Waiters. There was blanket excitement in this match and after missed chances and goalmouth incident galore, Bobby Charlton almost upstaged Law with two late goals. First, he took up an inside-forward position, despite still being fielded as a left-winger, to meet Moir's pass for a 20-yard shot. Minutes later, he surpassed himself, intercepting Waiters' throw-out, flicking the ball over his own shoulder and again letting Waiters watch the ball travel 20 yards before it hurtled past him and into his net.

After that 3-0 win over Blackpool, the importance of Law to the United team was illustrated most clearly by his absence through injury for the home match with second-placed West Bromwich Albion. This Law-less performance brought disorder to the United ranks. Without his promptings, Chisnall and Sadler often appeared to have forgotten their lines and Charlton went a-roving all over the front line in a largely unsuccessful effort to kick-start United's attacks.

Brought in to replace Law was 21-year-old Nobby Stiles and making his United debut in this game was a 17-year-old Belfast boy promoted from the youth team, George Best. He provided some of the brightest moments in a game that turned out to be a drab midfield battle. Best, indeed, began the move that brought the goal, passing inside to Stiles who, in turn, moved the ball inside of him for Sadler to take aim, fire and execute the shot that consigned West Brom to defeat and kept United top of the table.

Two days later, Moir was back in place of Best for the trip to Blackpool but Law was still missing. It still looked an easy two points for United: Blackpool were second-bottom of the First Division. There were, however, several changes in the Blackpool line-up from the earlier game at Old Trafford and their forward line was gingered up by a youngster named Alan Ball, who was making his sixth first-team appearance. After 20 minutes a powerful shot from him was parried by Gregg who made it a double save when he got to his feet to divert Quinn's stinging follow-up over the bar. Charlton then went close but in the 30th minute Gregg was beaten for what was to be the only goal of the game.

Those present had expected United to come back strongly. Instead, they remained under pressure for the rest of the match although Sadler went close on several occasions. United remained a point in the lead at the top of the First Division, pursued by West Brom, Nottingham Forest and Blackburn Rovers.

For United's next match, a visit to Highbury, Law, who had been doubtful up to kick-off, was back at inside-left. Gregg made a fine fourth-minute save from Brown and Arsenal made much of the early running before Herd, getting on the end of a swift move engineered by Charlton and Law, opened the scoring. Charlton then hit the Arsenal bar and Armstrong hit the United post. In the 26th minute Arsenal equalized. An abortive attempt at an offside trap let Strong in on goal and after Setters had tripped him, Eastham scored from the penalty spot.

Baker put Arsenal ahead eight minutes from the end but before the final whistle United were denied an equalizer by some fine saves on the part of Arsenal goalkeeper McKechnie. They were also unlucky scorers of one of the strangest non-goals of the 1960s. In 84 minutes a Charlton corner appeared to have curved straight into goal with McKechnie able only to push the ball into the rigging behind his post. The goalkeeper did knock the ball out into his six-yard box but he then lay dejected inside his goal as if in despair at failing to prevent the goal. It was only on hearing the yell of his right-half Brown to tell him that play was continuing that the goalkeeper jumped to his feet to block a follow-up shot from Law.

After that 2-1 defeat at Arsenal, United travelled to Rotterdam for their first European tie of the 1960s, a Cup-Winners' Cup meeting with Willem II Tilburg. Dutch football had only turned professional in the late 1950s. Willem II, in their first-ever European tie, were expected to be, at best, mere sparring partners for United before the British club encountered more hard-hitting European opposition. At the time of the tie, the part-timers of Willem II were mid-table in the Dutch First Division.

The match had been moved to the Feyenoord stadium in Rotterdam in anticipation of the crowd United were expected to draw. Willem II had increased their training to four nights a week and were on a bonus of £35 to win. They came close to earning some unexpected glory on an unhappy evening for United. United were described in the Dutch match programme notes as 'the personification of football' but they did little to enhance their reputation that evening.

Gregg and Foulkes were the only players in the United side who had represented United in their last European tie, against Milan in 1958. Only 20,000 were in the 62,000-capacity stadium and they saw Willem II go ahead after ten minutes. Koopal foxed Foulkes and slipped the ball to Louer, who beat Gregg. Two minutes later, Setters found Herd, who took advantage of hesitation on the part of the Dutch goalkeeper to equalize. Beforehand, Matt Busby had warned his players that they had to treat every match as a difficult one. To any who doubted him, that evening again proved how much sense the manager talked. Law hit a post 15 minutes from the end but later still,

George Best made his United debut in 1963. He found first-team football 'easy'.

27

Willem II nearly had that £35 win bonus when a shot from Louer came close to creeping under Gregg's body. Ten minutes from time, Herd was sent off by French referee Mr Tricot after a foul on Willem II left-back Brooymans. It ended 1-1.

United remained top of the First Division as they entered October but in their first game of the month, without Law, who had picked up an injury in Rotterdam, they were outplayed by Chelsea and were lucky to leave London with a 1-1 draw. They relinquished the League leadership to Tottenham who, further north in the capital, were beating Birmingham City 6-1.

The following Saturday, United were back on top, winning 1-0 at Bolton while Spurs drew at Sheffield United. At Bolton, United players had allowed themselves to be drawn into a series of running battles. With nine minutes remaining, Sadler sent the ball to Charlton on the wing and he had presented Herd with an uncomplicated opportunity for the only goal of the game.

Herd got another boost later that week when he discovered that he would be able to play against Willem II in the return Cup-Winners' Cup tie. UEFA's rules stated that a player sent off in the first leg of a European tie would be automatically suspended for the second leg but after representations from Willem II and the Dutch FA, the European governing body lifted the suspension. It was a sign of the times. There was still room for deeply sporting gestures such as that one despite mid-1960s fears that football was in danger of becoming over-commercialized after the abolition of the maximum wage for Britain's footballers in 1961.

The return with Willem II, played three weeks after the first leg, aroused enough curiosity among the Manchester public for 46,272 to turn up at Old Trafford. Two slick, well-worked goals, scored by Setters after seven minutes and Law after 12, put United firmly in control. Law scored a magnificent third, an effort that was, within minutes, almost matched by Cantwell but, unfortunately, the left-back's shot went flying past his own goalkeeper Gregg to make it 3-1 to United. A spectacular acrobatic effort from Charlton made it 4-1, Chisnall made it five, then Law tapped in the sixth after Herd had hit a post.

United had gone through to the next round in style. There they would need all the vim and vigour that had beaten Willem II at Old Trafford because their opponents were to be the Cup-Winners' Cup holders, Tottenham Hotspur. Spurs had become the first British club to win a European trophy in the spring of 1963 when they defeated Atletico Madrid 5-1 in the Cup-Winners' Cup final in Rotterdam. The Londoners had received a bye into the second round and, as First Division leaders, were strong favourites to win the tie.

On the day that draw was made, it was also announced that Old Trafford would be one of eight World Cup venues in England in 1966, hosting three matches in Group C. Goodison Park was to host the other three games in the group.

On 23 October, on another prestigious international occasion, Denis Law lined up alongside such players as Di Stefano, Puskas, Eusebio of Portugal and Yashin of the Soviet Union in a FIFA International Select. They were at Wembley to play England in a match to celebrate the centenary of the Football Association. Law was the only British player in FIFA's starting line-up, five of whom, FIFA announced beforehand, would be substituted at half-time to allow all 16 members of the squad to play. The FA still remained firmly against the use of substitutes but accepted this wish on the part of their guests 'while regretting it'. Bobby Charlton was Manchester United's representative in the England team.

A crowd of 100,000 paid approximately £90,000 in ticket money, record receipts for a match in Britain. Law was the outstanding man on the FIFA side. He provided numerous links between the middle of the field and the attack. He also scored FIFA's equalizer in 77 minutes, making it 1-1 after Di Stefano and Puskas had combined to create the chance. The goal was an extraordinary instance of Law's goalscoring abilities. Bearing down on Banks at speed, he corkscrewed his body over the ball to best disguise his intentions. He then uncoiled to release a shot that zipped past the England goalkeeper. In the 86th minute a Charlton shot was parried by FIFA's Yugoslavian goalkeeper Soskic and Greaves scored the winner from the rebound.

Three days later, United went into their match with West Ham at Old Trafford as First Division leaders. As well as having once more regained the lead from Tottenham, United were also the only side in the Football League with maximum points at home.

Organized superbly by Bobby Moore, West Ham defended in depth and got a 1-0 win. United, as against Willem II in Rotterdam, had looked baffled on meeting opponents who were unwilling to play as expansively as themselves. They were, as yet, just short of that magical element that would allow them to overwhelm the opposition through 90 minutes of variation and unpredictability in attack.

In their next two matches, a draw at home to Blackburn and a defeat at Wolves, United continued to look shaky. Law had gone four League games without scoring – an unusually long stretch for him. Less than 48 hours before United were due to meet Spurs in the League at Old Trafford, however, he scored four for Scotland at Hampden Park in a 6-1 win for his international side over Norway.

Graham Moore, a £35,000 signing from Chelsea earlier in the week, was inside-right against Tottenham on 9 November, replacing Phil Chisnall in the United line-up. From the start, United were on top. Herd hit the bar and Law had a goal disallowed for offside which Tottenham players admitted afterwards had looked legitimate to them. There was no need for United to conduct any angry post mortem, however. Even without that potential goal, they won easily.

Tony Dunne became a regular in the United team during the 1961-62 season. The Dublin-born defender could play equally well at either left or right full-back.

Law opened the scoring shortly before half-time despite being stretched out on the ground after a challenge for the ball. Herd made it two after a shot from the rampant Law had come to him via Danny Blanchflower's body. An own goal, conceded by Gregg when he punched a Greaves corner into his own net, made it 2-1 close to the end. But there was still time for Law, at his predatory best, to intercept two Tottenham passbacks and put some stylish polish on a fine afternoon's work, making it 4-1 to United on the afternoon and seven goals in less than two days for Denis Law.

A more disappointing contrast could hardly be found than between that and United's next match, away to Aston Villa. This time, Law left the pitch not in triumph but as one of the worst culprits in a disaster; sent off in a 4-0 defeat. Whereas United had been able to do no wrong against Tottenham, here they could do no right.

Villa were two up in 17 minutes and after 35 United were a man down. Law, as was often the case, had come in for some harsh treatment from the kick-off. He was to be observed at the scene of the crime as Deakin, Villa's right-half, fell to the ground holding his face. After an extended altercation on the field, Law departed. A dispute on the terraces followed with police intervening to stop the fighting there.

On 23 November, when United played host to Liverpool, the world was reeling from the assassination of US President John F Kennedy the previous day. It was a gloomy afternoon at Old Trafford. Gregg, challenged at a corner-kick by Liverpool's centre-back and captain Yeats, was badly injured. Strapped up, Gregg resumed in a position on the wing. He was later taken to hospital where a broken collar-bone was diagnosed and he sportingly absolved Yeats of any blame for the injury.

With 15 minutes of the match remaining, Yeats caused further injury to United when he got his head to a Callaghan corner to place the ball powerfully past Herd. The forward had taken over from Gregg in goal and had excelled.

It was a result that gave Liverpool the leadership of the First Division but only four points covered the top ten clubs. United had dropped from first to eighth place in a handful of games. They were now three points behind the Anfield side. However, despite the glut of clubs in their wake, Liverpool had looked so impressively well organized at Old Trafford that they appeared to be the best bet for the title.

Seven days later, United had recovered sufficiently to cruise to a 2-1 win over a Sheffield United side who had topped the table three weeks previously. Law, who had been subdued since his sending-off against Villa, was once again in lively form. The difference between the sides was in United's ability to pass and move intelligently while the Blades toiled manfully but with little real cleverness.

Once more it was Law who gave his team-mates the lead. For the first goal, after 20 minutes, Charlton took up a position at inside-left and switched the ball to Law who had flitted over to inside-right. He danced past three defenders before garnishing the move with a sweet finish. It was a goal that emphasised United's mobility, flexibility and improvisational powers.

The second goal was less picturesque but showed that United were not above the type of opportunism that is essential in football; Law snapped up a half-chance after Charlton's shot had been blocked by a Sheffield United defender. A late penalty, conceded by Setters, made it 2-1, a scoreline that failed to reflect the gulf between the sides.

It set United up nicely for the Cup-Winners' Cup first leg against Tottenham at White Hart Lane on 3 December. Once again, however, Law looked subdued. He had received severe criticism after his sending-off at Aston Villa and had a disciplinary hearing pending. Even so, with the score at 1-0 to Spurs, Law forced the London side's goalkeeper Brown into a fine save. White scored Spurs' second goal with just three minutes remaining. United had given a disciplined performance, backed up by Gaskell's inspired form in goal. It left them confident of their chances in the return at Old Trafford.

On the following Friday, 5 December, Law was suspended for 28 days, a punishment that was to take effect from 9 December. The FA Disciplinary Committee announced that the sentence had been passed after they had looked closely at Law's previous unsatisfactory discipline record. United would have to be prepared to be without him for the Cup-Winners' Cup second leg with Spurs, four League games and the third round of the FA Cup.

The next day Law signed off with four goals in a 5-2 home win over a Stoke City side that included Stanley Matthews. On leaving the field, Law was applauded by the 52,232 present, by his team-mates and by the Stoke players.

Law's showdown with English football's lawmen left United looking bereft of inspiration in the first half of the match with Spurs in the Cup-Winners' Cup the following Tuesday evening. Still, in seven minutes United did take the lead. Chisnall and Sadler cleverly worked the ball down the right and Herd met Sadler's cross with a well-judged diving header. Seconds later, Dave Mackay, Spurs' inspirational half-back, broke a leg in a challenge with Cantwell but Spurs remained the more impressive side for the rest of that half. The Londoners would have equalized but for a goal-line clearance by Cantwell.

Twelve minutes after half-time, United equalized on aggregate when Herd flicked the ball into the net from close range. Greaves, however, put Spurs back into the lead on aggregate shortly afterwards and the teams were reduced to ten apiece when Setters left the field with blood streaming from a gash in his head.

Smith missed an excellent chance for Spurs then Charlton shot over the bar from close-range. Charlton, who had started the match on the left wing, had by then moved inside, and that had coincided with United upgrading their performance by a considerable degree. In the absence of Law, Charlton supplied the type of inspiration that was the usual province of the Scot.

With ten minutes remaining, Crerand flighted a long ball to Charlton, who twisted on to it to make the score 3-1 to United. With the teams locked on aggregate and a replay at Villa Park looming, Crerand and Charlton again joined forces for Charlton to hit the winner. Now 4-1 down, Spurs had been left with mere seconds in which to respond. They couldn't.

Back in the League, a mid-December win over Sheffield Wednesday put United two points behind new leaders Tottenham and Blackburn, who had displaced Liverpool. But four days before Christmas Everton put a hole in United's championship chances with a 4-0 win on a day when, Charlton excepted, United's forwards were signally lacking in invention. Such a charge could rarely be levelled at George Best who played his second first-team game on 28 December. That was two days after United had been on the end of another drubbing, this time 6-1 at Burnley. That left United in sixth place, six points behind leaders Blackburn.

George Best's dark, brooding good looks made him one of the faces of the 1960s in Britain.

At Burnley, United had been thoroughly belittled and it was all too much for Crerand, who was sent from the field 13 minutes from time after appearing to elbow Burnley's outside-left Towers in the face. Willie Morgan, an 18-year-old Scot, had shown some breathtaking skills on the Burnley right wing. He scored twice and was singled out for special congratulations at the end of the match by Setters. United had fielded a strange formation with Bobby Charlton at centre-forward although he did look comfortable in that position. Left-back Brennan looked a good deal less happy at outside-left.

Two days later, United came close to reversing the Boxing Day result when they met Burnley in the rematch at Old Trafford. Best had been enjoying Christmas with his family in Belfast and when United asked him to return to England for this match he insisted on being transported back home immediately afterwards. When United agreed to fly him both ways he knew he had hit the big time. Best had joined the club in 1961, travelling from Belfast to Manchester with another youngster called Eric McMordie. After one day at Old Trafford, they decided they would not

31

make it at such a big club and returned to Belfast. Best's father immediately telephoned Matt Busby and within a fortnight the 15-year-old was back in Manchester determined to prove himself.

Best lined up on the left wing, much to fellow Irishman Brennan's relief. On the right wing was Liverpudlian Willie Anderson, making his debut at the age of 16. The two youngsters freshened up the United attack. Each received equal praise for their efforts that afternoon, justifying Busby's brave decision to have a fling with youth.

Of the more experienced players, the defenders had one or two shaky moments, taking a pounding from Burnley at the beginning of each half. Half-backs Setters and Crerand, however, controlled play throughout. Charlton again looked pleased with the greater degree of involvement that playing at centre-forward entailed.

After Herd had opened the scoring from an acute angle in the 11th minute, Anderson found Moore with a corner for the second. Best got the third, calmly stroking the ball into the net after Charlton had miskicked on the edge of the six-yard box. Moore made it 4-0 midway through the second half after Gaskell had made several assured saves. Crerand supplied Herd with the opportunity to make it 5-0 before Burnley got a late goal.

Best and Anderson were in an unchanged side that travelled to Southampton for United's next match, an FA Cup third-round tie. It looked a simple assignment for the cup-holders against the Second Division side. But by half-time United were 2-0 down with their two young wingers struggling badly. In the second half, however, with Crerand again at his best, United snapped back into life.

After 51 minutes, Crerand sent young Anderson on an errand up the wing and he delivered a cross for Moore to head United's first goal of the afternoon. An own goal from Southampton's Traynor brought the equalizer. Eight minutes from the end, Anderson found Crerand and he eluded three defenders to score the winner. United's superior teamwork – as evidenced in the previous season's FA Cup – had seen them through yet again.

A surprise home defeat to Birmingham City on Law's return in mid-January was another setback in the championship race. Charlton had been missing through injury but he was back the following week when a 4-1 win over West Brom kept United still within hailing distance of the top clubs. At the Hawthorns, several players wore basketball boots to obtain a better grip on the slippery surface. It was the first time Law, Best and Charlton had played in the same side. All three scored; Law getting two goals, the others one apiece.

Best's goal, the second, was the best of the day. He took a neat pass from Law, angled himself clear of the West Brom defence and then squeezed the ball neatly between the posts from the tightest of angles. Anderson had failed to match the Irishman's progress and had been left out of the team for the previous week's match against Birmingham.

A Law hat-trick, on a day when he was back on peak form, knocked the stuffing out of Third Division Bristol Rovers in a fourth-round cup tie at Old Trafford, United winning 4-1. For United's third goal, Law had run close to 60 yards before getting his head to a cross from Charlton.

Two late goals earned United a 3-1 home League win over an Arsenal side for whom Ian Ure was outstanding at centre-back, as he had been in the fixture at Highbury. League-leaders Tottenham remained within United's sights. The following midweek the British Olympic football team warmed up for their match with Greece with an outing against United's second string at Old Trafford; United won 4-0.

On 8 February, the day after the British and French governments had announced they would be building a channel tunnel by the end of the

1960s, United lost 3-2 to Leicester. Best had a goal disallowed and Charlton hit the bar in the closing minutes. Best was still on the left wing with Charlton at centre-forward and Law in between. Hesitant moments in defence had lost United the points.

An all-ticket crowd of over 38,000 was at Barnsley to see the local side face United in the fifth round of the FA Cup. Stiles, who had been in and out of the team since his debut, replaced Moore at inside-right. Herd was on the right wing. United coasted to a 4-0 win with Best getting two of the goals. Stiles' energetic performance was a convincing argument for him to be given an extended run in the team.

Best had quickly shown he had the required temperament for top-class football. Law and Charlton were fantastically direct in hunting for goals; Best would follow his own nose. Often he would appear to have gone too

Sporting Lisbon goalkeeper Carvalho (below left) is grounded as Denis Law scores the opening goal in their Cup-Winners' Cup tie at Old Trafford.
Law (below) scores United's fourth goal against Sporting, from the penalty spot.

far in his athletic cunning but he would almost always find a speedy solution. United's fans were soon convinced they were seeing a player who was the very best; what was puzzling was how he could be so much better than the competition.

A natural athlete and a natural footballer, Best was as close to a force of nature as Britain has ever seen on a football field. As his reputation quickly grew, he came under increasing pressure from his markers but his football subsequently grew greater in grace. His startling shimmies, kaleidoscopic selection of moves and instantaneous bursts of pace left even the most accomplished opponents scything the air.

'I did have this quality of being able to sway around players like a matador,' he said. 'That was due to my great sense of balance. It is the most important quality if you want to be able to ride challenges. If that bull is rushing at you at 100 miles an hour and you've got to get out of the way, you need balance. I had perfect balance from an early age. I never had to think about the angle that a player was coming in at me; I simply used to adjust myself. It takes a sort of bravery as well, to take on people when you know they will try and clobber you.'

The classic image of Best is of him sashaying round an opponent on the wing. But he was a fully rounded footballer. He could use both feet equally effectively, he was an excellent header of the ball and he was hard and fast in the tackle. He also had a sensual appetite for the game.

A rearranged midweek League match at Old Trafford on 19 February found United teasing Bolton Wanderers, winning 5-0 to remain in touch at the top. Best, Law and Charlton had quickly reached a fine understanding and in this match they were ably backed up by a fine supporting cast starring Stiles, Setters and Herd.

In the quarter-finals of the Cup-Winners' Cup, the first leg of which was scheduled for 26 February, United were to meet Sporting Lisbon, the Portuguese cup-holders. On the preceding Saturday, United continued their steady progress in the League. Facing Blackburn Rovers, one of the teams that had made the running for the title, they survived sustained Blackburn pressure for most of the first half. United then took a lucky half-time lead after Chisnall's shot had taken the right turning at the foot of a post.

Blackburn equalized deservedly midway through the second half. But regardless of how well United or their opponents played on any given day, Denis Law was always likely to impose his will on a match. Here, he swooped on a Crerand pass close to the halfway line before gliding away from the Blackburn defence and shooting home from 25 yards. A minute later, he accepted another pass from Crerand to score the third, decisive goal. United remained serious contenders for a treble of the League and two cups.

During the opening stages of United's first leg with Sporting Lisbon at Old Trafford, the Portuguese indulged in the type of elaborate trickery that helped make European evenings so special. But midway through the first half it was United who took the lead. Law took a pass from Charlton, threaded his way round two defenders and lifted the ball over Sporting goalkeeper Carvalho as he advanced from his line. Six minutes from half-time, Law and Charlton reversed their earlier roles, Law setting Charlton free to beat Carvalho with a cleanly-struck shot.

It seemed certain to be United's night when, on the hour, a penalty was awarded to them for a challenge on Stiles. It looked a soft award but Law didn't worry about that as he made it 3-0. A 25-yard shot from Osvaldo brought Sporting a 66th minute goal but United were given another penalty a few minutes later. The Portuguese club's players indulged in long and bitter protests over the decision – Charlton had appeared to have lost the ball when he was adjudged to have been tripped by a Sporting defender. The referee stood by his ruling and Law made it 4-1.

Despite the controversy surrounding United's two penalties, the emphatic scoreline left United's players and the 60,000-plus crowd confident they would advance to the semi-finals after they had contested the second leg in Lisbon three weeks later.

An all-ticket 64,000 crowd rolled up on the following Saturday for the FA Cup's tie of the sixth round: United against Sunderland at Old Trafford. Sunderland, the Second Division leaders, had been playing an impressive passing game all season. They did so again at Old Trafford, so much so that, with five minutes remaining, they were 3-1 ahead, having earlier gone 3-0 up ten minutes after half-time. Law had made it 3-1, then Charlton made it 3-2 with five minutes to go. Finally, Best lit up the dying embers of the match by carefully finding a route for his shot that enabled it to bypass several Sunderland bodies as it found its way to goal.

The replay at Roker Park ended 1-1 after 90 minutes thanks only to a late equalizer from Law. Early in extra-time, Sunderland went ahead again and Law hit the bar three minutes from the end of the extra period. But two minutes from time, Herd picked out Charlton who headed the goal that got United an equalizer and a second replay.

At the neutral venue of Leeds Road, Huddersfield, Sunderland, as was becoming the established pattern in this tie, opened the scoring. On this occasion, the goal came three minutes after half-time but within seconds Law had equalized. Chisnall, a minute later, made it 2-1. Three minutes after that, Law increased United's lead further with a penalty. On the hour, Best, Charlton and Law combined to make it four, then Herd made it 5-1 to United. The 55,000 crowd had seen United break the deadlock in no uncertain terms. The only blot on an excellent evening was a disorderly free-for-all among the players near the end of the match.

It put United in the semi-final, to be played at Hillsborough on 14 March. There they would face West Ham United for the second successive Saturday, United having beaten the Londoners 2-0 in a League match at Upton Park. That win had been achieved despite United missing Charlton, Best, Law, Setters and Foulkes through injury. Crerand, as in the second replay with Sunderland on 9 March, had orchestrated the win.

The injured who had missed the first match with West Ham were back in place for the semi-final, making United firm favourites to win. But a heavy playing surface at Hillsborough contributed to a leaden-footed, sluggish performance against a West Ham side led by Bobby Moore. After a nerve-racking first half, in which the Londoners had gone close on several occasions, West Ham were 2-0 up by the 65th minute. Law got one back before Moore gave Hurst the chance to score West Ham's third.

Hopes of a treble having been confounded, United were immediately plunged into the second leg of their tie with Sporting Lisbon in the Estadio de Jose Alvalade. Within two minutes, justice, in Portuguese eyes, was seen to be done in return for the penalties that had been awarded against them at Old Trafford. Dunne was ruled to have handled inside the penalty area. Osvaldo took the penalty-kick and scored. After 13 minutes, United's aggregate lead, which had looked so secure, began looking precarious when Osvaldo bundled in the second.

A minute into the second half, Geo made it 3-0. The Sporting players darted here and there quickly and imaginatively all night and they took the overall lead in the tie in considerable style: Mascarenhas leapt athletically to hitch-kick the ball to Morais who drilled in the fourth. And less than ten minutes after half-time, Osvaldo lined up a 35-yard free-kick and planted it past Gaskell. It was the last goal of the evening, making it 5-0 to Sporting and leaving United out and very down.

It had been United's heaviest defeat in Europe. From appearing assured of a famous victory, their self-confidence had taken a serious pummelling. It left to United the sole target of the League title and the first Saturday in April looked like giving United a strong indication of how realistic their title expectations were. They travelled to Anfield to face League leaders Liverpool. Liverpool were top with 50 points from 36 games, a point above Everton. United went into the game on the back of an eight-game unbeaten run in the League which had yielded them 13 points out of a possible 16. They now had 47 points from 37 games. A win was vital but they didn't get it. Liverpool won 3-0 in impressive style to present United with their third major disappointment in three weeks.

United would go on to finish second in the League, four points behind Liverpool. West Ham won the FA Cup while Sporting Lisbon took the European Cup-Winners' Cup. In all three competitions, United had been second only to the winners but those who had watched them over the season realized that the football they were witnessing was anything but second-best. It had been a vibrant, excitement-filled season for United. Few doubted that this solid, shapely side would be any less entertaining in the 1964-65 season.

The Beatles began to achieve widespread public recognition in 1963, the year in which the 1960s began to swing for United. Although none of the group were fanatical football followers, Matt Busby did receive a mention on the Beatles' final album Let It Be, *which was recorded in early 1969. In the song 'Dig It', John Lennon invokes Busby's name along with several others, including those of the blues-singer BB King and the actress Doris Day.*

Harold Wilson, the populist politician who would soon be elected Britain's prime minister, was kicking a ball about on a Scilly Isles beach two days before the 1964-65 season began. Wilson was on his annual holiday but Matt Busby, a genuine football man, was already at work making crucial long-term decisions for Manchester United as could be seen in his line-up for the opening League match of the season. Nobby Stiles had moved to left-half and his place at inside-right had been filled by Bobby Charlton. Herd had returned to centre-forward and on the right wing was John Connelly, an English international newly signed from Burnley for £60,000. George Best was still on the left wing where he had spent most of the previous season. Denis Law remained at inside-left.

David Gaskell was in goal; Shay Brennan and Tony Dunne were the full-backs. The impassive figure of Bill Foulkes, starting his 14th season at Old Trafford, held things together in the centre of the defence. Pat Crerand was missing for the first two League matches but he would be Busby's first-choice for right-half throughout the season. After the opening five League matches, Pat Dunne, an Irish goalkeeper signed for £10,500 from Shamrock Rovers, replaced Gaskell in goal for the remainder of the season. Those 11 players would form the backbone of the United side for season 1964-65. Others such as Sadler, Moir, Cantwell and Setters would be brought in for a game or two but usually only when injuries or suspensions hit the regulars.

'The only instruction that Busby ever gave really was: "We know you can play football. Go out and play the type of football that you can play. And no matter what the result is at the end of the game if you've tried your best I can ask for no more." It was as simple as that,' said Denis Law.

'Many, many times when they tried something that didn't come off,' said Busby, 'I was quite happy, because that's the right thing to do. I was always very happy that they were a creative side, building up creation rather than destruction.'

In the first match of the season, at home to West Brom that August, the Hawthorns side took the lead in the first half. Connelly soon showed his worth, however, curving over a cross that Law headed into goal as if releasing four months of pent-up energy. Charlton then staked a claim to remain in a central position when he sent one of his custom-built long-range specials into the West Brom net. West Brom equalized before half-time with an offside-looking goal and struck a post in the second half before the match ended 2-2. United had produced some excellent football but the fans went home worried that some of the old inconsistencies were still there.

A visit to cup-holders West Ham followed and Best, Law and Herd went close to scoring after the Londoners had taken a fourth-minute lead. It became 2-0 after 20 minutes and although United battled back to make it 2-1, West Ham sealed the win with a third goal. At one point, early in the second half, Law had looked skywards, as if pleading for divine intervention, after a shot had rolled just the wrong side of a West Ham post. United had played some scintillating football in their opening two games but had taken only one point out of a possible four. Perhaps this was just not going to be United's year, regardless of the quality of their football.

For the trip to Leicester on the second Saturday of the season, Crerand was back at right-half while Sadler was at centre-forward. After two

minutes, Law collided with Mr Wells, the referee, who required extensive treatment. Two minutes from the end, Law delivered a similarly heavy blow to Leicester, firing home Best's cross. Best had also supplied Sadler with the ball for the first United goal in the 2-2 draw.

The first victory of the season arrived the following week when the extra dimension that wingers Best and Connelly added to United's play proved too much for West Ham at Old Trafford. Best, Law and Charlton combined to give Connelly a simple opening goal. Law made it two, tapping home the rebound after a thunderous shot from Connelly had forced Standen, the West Ham goalkeeper, into a fine save. Best finished the scoring with a hard-hit, accurate shot to make it 3-1.

Still United proved to be erratic. A 2-1 defeat at Fulham was followed by a 3-3 draw at Everton. This was not championship form. United were synonymous with splendid entertainment – the Everton game had contained superb goals by Law, Connelly and Herd. But they were also a bit of an easy touch at times, occasionally failing to tighten up defensively as well as they ought to have done.

Those results were followed by an easy 3-0 home win over Nottingham

John Connelly, an outside-right, joined United from Burnley in the summer of 1964. He contributed 20 goals to the United cause in the 1964-65 season, making him third-top goalscorer behind Denis Law and David Herd.

Forest. Then two wonderful goals brought a 2-1 win over Everton as United's settled selection started to gel and push towards the top of the League. For the first of the goals against Everton, Best took a Crerand pass. He then shimmied away from several Everton defenders and sent a shot into the top corner of the Everton goal. Not to be outdone, Law improved on Best's effort with a 45-yard run that was capped by a magnificent shot.

By finishing second in the League the previous spring, United had qualified for the Inter-Cities Fairs Cup. This tournament had originally been established as a European competition for clubs representing cities that held a trade fair. By the mid-1960s, however, it had become the European tournament for sides who had finished in the League places immediately below the champions. The standard of competition, therefore, was extremely high. From 1972 onwards it would become known as the UEFA Cup.

A tiny crowd greeted United for their first Fairs Cup tie when they travelled to Sweden to play Djurgarden, a club based on one of the islands that are part of Stockholm. Performing in front of only 6,537 spectators may have unnerved the United players, as they went 1-0 behind to a Johansson goal after just eight minutes. There were only three minutes remaining when Herd headed the equalizer from Connelly's cross and saved United a certain amount of ignominy.

United were their usual selves the following Saturday when they met Tottenham at Old Trafford. In a flurry of activity before half-time, Law twice hit the crossbar and had a goal disallowed. He accompanied each dramatic piece of action with his own theatrics. United were rewarded for their dominance, however, when Crerand opened the scoring with a crisp left-footed shot from 20 yards. Crerand scored more luckily after half-time, his shot dodging through Jennings' hands. Then Law, inevitably, added another dramatic moment, scoring the third despite having looked offside. Law hit the woodwork again before scoring with an opportunist effort to give United a 4-1 victory.

George Best said that the two players whose names he always looked for first on the team sheet were those of Crerand and Stiles. Crerand's passing kept everything moving while Stiles was the hard man that every team had to have.

By mid-October, United's League challenge had righted itself. They were now back on course for the championship, two points behind the leaders Chelsea, a young side managed by Tommy Docherty and including Terry Venables at half-back. United had beaten Chelsea at Stamford Bridge in front of 60,000 the previous month. A goal in each half from Best and Law had shown which of the two sides possessed the sort of style required of potential champions. United had left the field to a standing ovation.

'George scored a goal that night that I just stood and applauded,' said Pat Crerand. 'He changed feet so quickly and hit a screamer into the top corner. His performance was as good as Alfredo Di Stefano's for Real Madrid against Eintracht Frankfurt, one of the great individual performances of all time.'

Aston Villa were at Old Trafford on 24 October. After 18 minutes Connelly's hard-hit cross was directed into the net by Herd. Two minutes later Best hypnotized a Villa defender before sending the ball into Law's path for a 20-yard classic. Law and Best were in transcendental form and Law made it 3-0 in 52 minutes with another 20-yarder. Five minutes on, Connelly knocked in the rebound after the ball had come back off the crossbar. Inside the final half-hour, Law took Crerand's pass, rounded the goalkeeper and sent the ball into the net. Then Herd made it 6-0 with a powerful shot. With seconds remaining, Law, still hungry, got his head to a cross from Stiles that had reached him in awkward fashion, to make it 7-0. It was United's equal-biggest win of the 1960s.

It had been by no means a one-sided contest. On several occasions, Villa had tested Dunne but United had shown just how emphatically they would win when the breaks did go their way; a four-goal winning margin might more accurately have reflected the way play had gone. With Chelsea drawing at Tottenham, it brought United to within a point of the leaders.

On 27 October, Djurgarden, who had just become Swedish champions, were welcomed to Old Trafford for the second leg of the Fairs Cup tie. They gave a disciplined defensive performance and, initially, United struggled to break them down. After 20 minutes, however, United worked an elaborate free-kick 25 yards from goal. Law dummied the ball and Charlton sidefooted it to Herd. He then found the running Law who did look marginally offside as he opened the scoring. From there, United motored on to a 6-1 win. Pick of the goals was the fifth one, Charlton bobbing and weaving from the halfway line before scoring.

On the final day of October, United visited their northern rivals Liverpool at Anfield, where United had finally lost their chance of the League title six months previously. After 35 minutes, Charlton crossed from the left and Law headed the ball downwards. Liverpool defender Byrne tried to clear but the ball came to Herd who crashed it into the Liverpool net. Midway through the second half, United got a second. Crerand took the ball for a lengthy run, passed it to Law, then waited for the return which he lobbed cleverly over Liverpool goalkeeper Lawrence.

It was an accomplished performance by United with Crerand at the hub of almost everything good on display. He even made a vital goal-line clearance late in the match. On the same afternoon, Chelsea lost 1-0 to Burnley. United leapt a point ahead of the Stamford Bridge side at the top of the First Division, just-reward for their sustained burst of style during that early autumn.

A win over Sheffield Wednesday kept United on top. They then flew to West Germany to meet Borussia Dortmund in the second round of the

Borussia Dortmund winger Emmerich puts Manchester United goalkeeper Pat Dunne under pressure in the first leg of their Fairs Cup tie in Dortmund.

Fairs Cup. 'It's going to be a very hard match,' said Matt Busby on arrival with the United party. 'I saw the Borussia players two weeks ago. They're good.' Borussia had been German champions in 1963 and had reached the semi-finals of the European Cup in the spring of 1964, losing narrowly to eventual winners Internazionale. Two weeks before their match with United, they had been top of the Bundesliga.

In the opening five minutes of the match in Germany, United found themselves being put under severe pressure. Law deflected a Bayer shot off the line after the Scot had seen the necessity of getting back to help out the United defence.

United retaliated with two Charlton attempts on goal that went

close to getting them the opener and in 12 minutes United did go ahead. Law juggled the ball with head and foot before releasing Herd whose confident finish made it 1-0. United – in particular Charlton, Best and Law – got into their stride immediately after that. Charlton devastated the 25,000 crowd by scoring with a shot that hit the underside of the Dortmund bar on its way into the net.

Five minutes after half-time, Best slalomed his way through the Dortmund defence to make it 3-0. Two minutes later, a mistimed tackle by Crerand on Kurrat resulted in a penalty that Kurrat converted. Best was continually picking away at the Dortmund defence and in 77 minutes he crossed for Law to head a fourth goal. United were not finished; Charlton got two goals in the final ten minutes to give him a hat-trick and United a 6-1 win.

The Saturday afterwards, United achieved a useful 2-1 victory at Blackpool. United had managed to do without Best, who was in Lausanne playing for Northern Ireland in a World Cup tie that they lost 2-1 to Switzerland. The day was marred, however, by the sending-off of Law. The player had appeared keen to create a record for the lengthiest piece of dissent seen in the First Division. He had continually pestered the referee with his opinions after being penalized for an elbowing incident involving Blackpool's Ball. The referee, who initially had been planning to book Law, then sent him off.

BOBBY CHARLTON
MANCHESTER UNITED
CENTRE FORWARD

Bottles rained down on the pitch, a common sight in the 1960s whenever the crowd disliked what they saw on the field of play. Afterwards, Mr Rhodes, the referee, said: 'A referee has his responsibilities, and it is no use his shirking them.' Law had behaved well since his severe encounter with the disciplinary authorities in December 1963. However, going back to upbraid a referee three times seemed almost like a plea to be sent off, especially when the referee in question had his notebook out. It appeared irresponsible on the part of Busby's captain.

On the final day of November, United turned on the style in front of 60,000 at Highbury. Law showed he was in no way depressed after the previous week's events. After four minutes, Connelly's corner was nodded to Law by Charlton. In an instant, the Scot had knocked in the opener and was acknowledging the crowd's plaudits with his trademark wave. Connelly made it two. Then Law, just before the half-hour, again took centre-stage with some aplomb. A cutting through-ball from Charlton found Best. He injected some confusion into the Arsenal defence before flicking the ball to Law who ended the move in the fashion it deserved with a sweet half-volley on the turn.

Arsenal pulled two goals back but the news that Chelsea had lost at home south of the Thames made this one of the most satisfying afternoons of the season. Those results meant that United moved three points clear of Chelsea at the top.

Four days later, Borussia Dortmund's players turned up at Old Trafford for the second leg of their Fairs Cup tie. There was to be no respite for the Germans. In the first minute a Charlton special from 20 yards flew past Tilkowski for the first goal of the night. Goals from Charlton, Law and Connelly completed the formalities as United went into the next round on a 10-1 aggregate.

Tilkowski and Charlton would come face to face again in the 1966 World Cup final. At the time of the Dortmund match, however, Charlton's England future was by no means certain. Alf Ramsey continued to use him on the left wing long after he had become well established as an inside-forward for United.

At the end of the match with Dortmund, the 32,000 present applauded the Germans as they left the pitch in recognition of their non-stop effort. This was not a bunch of gallant losers, though: it is a further measure of United's achievements in these two matches that Dortmund would win the West German Cup in 1965. They would then go on to take the 1966 European Cup-Winners' Cup, beating Liverpool in the final at Hampden Park.

The following Saturday, the players of United and Leeds United were led off the Old Trafford pitch after it had become obscured by heavy fog. After a ten-minute break, during which the fog lifted, play between the sides recommenced. The match ended in a 1-0 win for Leeds. Their centre-half, Jack Charlton, had thwarted the bright ideas of his brother Bobby and his United team-mates. It was United's first defeat in three months and, the unfavourable intervention of the elements notwithstanding, a desperately unlucky one. Best had hit the crossbar before retiring injured and a number of fine saves by Leeds' goalkeeper Sprake had kept their goal intact.

The following Friday, 11 December, the news that Old Trafford had dreaded came when Law was again suspended for 28 days, starting from 14 December. He also received a £50 fine. For the second consecutive Christmas and New Year, United would be tested as to how well they could cope without their talisman.

The next day, West Brom held United to a 1-1 draw at the Hawthorns. Chelsea went top again on goal average. Law's last performance for a month was one of verve, imagination and... a goal. Another draw, at home to Birmingham in midweek, put United back on top although Chelsea now had a game in hand.

Frost and mist saw United's next game, at home to Leicester, called off. While United were idle, Chelsea lost to Sunderland. Leeds, with a win over Wolves, joined United at the top on 34 points. Nottingham Forest were fourth on 28 points. After the matches at Christmas and New Year, Leeds were two points clear of United while Chelsea were level with them.

In the third round of the FA Cup, Fourth Division Chester City took a 1-0 half-time lead at Old Trafford and United were forced to struggle for their eventual 2-1 victory.

Law signalled his return to the United side in the same manner in which he had left it, scoring twice in the 2-2 draw at Nottingham Forest's City Ground on 16 January. Leeds also drew, keeping them a point ahead of Chelsea and two points clear of United.

For the second successive season, United were drawn to face English opposition in European competition. In their third-round Fairs Cup tie, Everton were to be their opponents. The first leg, at Old Trafford on 20 January, left little to be desired in terms of United's overall performance. Law did look a little ring-rusty but Best and Charlton were immense, as were the half-back team of Crerand and Stiles. Only the goalkeeping of Everton's West matched United's attacking efforts.

After United had already gone close on several occasions it was Everton who took the lead in the 14th minute. Foulkes mistimed a clearance and Pickering, Everton's centre-forward, streaked clear to shoot past a static Pat Dunne. United equalized in 33 minutes when Gabriel made a hash of a pass-back to West. Connelly got between the two Everton men to score. It remained 1-1, ensuring that the return at Goodison Park three weeks later would be intriguing.

Two ultra-defensive performances from a Stoke City side that by then included Maurice Setters and Dennis Viollet saw United held to draws in cup and League on successive Saturdays. In the cup replay at Old Trafford United made and missed a series of chances. Finally, Herd, in a crouching position, got to Dunne's cross to put United in the next round.

A disappointing 1-0 defeat at Tottenham preceded United's trip to Goodison Park for the second leg of their Fairs Cup tie. In front of 55,000, United wasted little time in getting a grip on the game. Six minutes had gone when Connelly played a one-two with Law before speeding off for his second goal of the tie. A superb save by West prevented Connelly making it a hat-trick over the two legs. Then Pickering's free-kick came back off a United post. Connelly had a goal disallowed for hands before Pickering, with the aid of a deflection, equalized for Everton.

As in the first match between the sides, the quality of the football was faultless. It was United who got the deciding goal, however, after Law had set Connelly free once more. His shot was half-stopped by West and Herd, following up, made it 2-1. United had come out on top in another domestic dispute.

Two home wins over Burnley on successive Saturdays, in the League then in the cup, kept United moving forward. In the cup-tie, United were trailing 1-0 seven minutes from the end against a Burnley side employing an eight-man defence. It required a touch of unorthodoxy to sway matters in United's favour. Best was the man to provide it. His boot had come off and, when the ball came to him he was still clutching his footwear. That did not prevent him moving the ball on with his stocking-soled foot to Crerand. The right-half's chipped ball to Law inspired an overhead kick for the equalizer. A minute later, Crerand, with a 30-yard shot, got the winner.

'As to whether we play it off the cuff,' Busby was to say, 'well, we always hold tactical talks every week and before every match. But we do encourage individualism, especially that of Best, Charlton and Law. Unless you encourage that sort of individualism then you really have nothing. The players, of course, have to fit into the working pattern but use their basic skills as best they can.'

A miserable 1-0 defeat at Sunderland on 24 February left United three points behind Chelsea and Leeds with all three having played 30 games. Once again that season United were due to play the same opponents in League and cup in successive weeks. A simple 3-0 win over those opponents, relegation strugglers Wolves, helped United make up some ground in the League. Snow and ice caused the cup tie at Molineux to be postponed but when it was played United ran out classy 5-3 winners.

Racing driver Jim Clark became the first man to lap Brands Hatch at over 100 mph on 13 March, the day League-leaders Chelsea appeared at Old Trafford. United were also ready to increase the pace of the First Division race.

After just three minutes the Londoners were being put firmly in their place – and it wasn't at the top of the division. An easy-looking clearance for right-back McCreadie was charged down by Best. The ball fell kindly for the defender but Best, being held off by McCreadie, again got a foot to the ball. The ball still looked to be McCreadie's but, unnerved by Best's persistence, he fell as he tried to scramble the ball to a team-mate. From close to the goal-line Best instantaneously arced the ball over goalkeeper Bonetti, who had looked to have blocked all routes to goal. Few players would even have seen the chance; fewer still had Best's debonair ability to turn it into a goal. Best's control over the ball made it look simple.

Best's Beatlesque appearance attracted attention and adulation. He would not have looked out of place on the cover of the band's 1965 album *Rubber Soul*. He might have felt more at home there than among the short-back-and-sided footballers of the mid-1960s – it would be the late 1960s before other young footballers began to grow their hair. Best was receiving up to 1,000 fan letters a week, mainly from teenage girls. He was attractive to women and found their company soothing in between being rammed and battered by embarrassed defenders. 'The birds kept me sane,' he said.

Two goals from Herd either side of half-time and one by Law polished off the Londoners. Chelsea had barely been able to mount an attack all afternoon. The 4-0 win left United a point behind Chelsea and Leeds.

A superb 4-1 win at Fulham on 15 March was followed by a 1-0 defeat at Sheffield Wednesday five days later, leaving United again three points behind the leaders, Leeds. The heavy Hillsborough pitch had not been conducive to United's touch players. Ominously, they had to return to the same venue the following Saturday, 27 March, for an FA Cup semi-final with Leeds.

Denis Law keeps his eye on the ball as it enters the net in United's 5-0 win over Blackburn Rovers at Ewood Park in April 1965.

Earlier that season, United's League encounters with Fulham and Everton had been pockmarked by brawling among the players. This FA Cup semi-final proved most memorable for an incident on the hour when half-a-dozen players got involved in a set-to. It was the climax of an afternoon on which a combination of lenient refereeing and malicious tackling had rendered the football impotent, as reflected in the 0-0 scoreline.

Leeds, under manager Don Revie, 'enjoyed' a reputation as a team of hard players. But with individuals such as Law, Foulkes, Stiles and Crerand in their side United also knew how to look after themselves.

After the first match, both sides were heavily criticized in the media for their conduct. The replay, at the City Ground, Nottingham, on 31 March, produced a total of 55 fouls. United still established superiority. They created a clutch of chances in either half but failed to score. With a minute remaining, and the score 0-0, Leeds' Bremner beat Pat Dunne with a header and United were out of the cup.

The sides were scheduled to meet again in a League clash at Elland Road on the Saturday of the Easter weekend. It would be a match that would go a long way towards deciding the ultimate destination of the title. In between, United had been pepped up by their 5-0 thrashing of Blackburn at Ewood Park on 3 April, which had included a Charlton hat-trick. On 12 April, United beat Leicester 1-0 at Old Trafford. 'We were gutted,' said Nobby Stiles on the aftermath of the Leeds cup-tie. 'But

Manchester United right-back Shay Brennan blocks an attempt on goal by Leeds United's Albert Johanneson in the 1965 FA Cup semi-final at Hillsborough in March 1965. Goalkeeper Pat Dunne prepares to intervene.

A linesman comes to the assistance of Mr Windle, the referee, at the end of the FA Cup semi-final replay between Leeds and Manchester United. He had been knocked to the ground when the crowd invaded the pitch and a spectator punched him on the back of the head.

Bobby Charlton was the best. In the next game, against Blackburn, he played them on his own and scored three. His spirit lifted us.'

Leeds were unbeaten since November as they prepared to meet United on 17 April but that record held little fear for the Manchester club. Again they proved that when it came to a contest on purely footballing terms they would, more often than not, emerge as winners. Their superior passing skills, embodied by Crerand and Stiles, helped them outmanoeuvre Leeds in every part of the field. A decisive finishing shot from Connelly, after Tony Dunne and Law had carefully engineered the opportunity for him, was all that separated the sides. But as in the match with Chelsea five weeks previously, United had decisively demonstrated which team deserved to be champions.

On Easter Monday, 19 April, United went top, winning 4-2 at Birmingham City while both Chelsea and Leeds lost. It left United a point clear of their two rivals with three games to play.

In the first of those games, on 24 April, United met Liverpool at Old Trafford. Five minutes from half-time, Law chested down a loose clearance and found the back of the net in quick, businesslike fashion. Early in the second half, Law met Crerand's low, hard cross with the same result. In celebrating, Law followed the ball into the net where he gashed his knee on a stanchion. He then had to leave the field to have three stitches to the wound. With less than ten minutes remaining, Crerand hit a powerful shot that Connelly diverted goalwards to make it 3-0 for a thoroughly convincing rout of the soon-to-be-deposed champions.

Two days later, on 26 April, Law, known to the United fans as the King of Old Trafford, and his team-mates, the aristocracy of English football, were crowned champions of England. It made official what everyone knew already – United were the best team in the country. The almost-complete, new cantilevered stand on the United Road side of the ground, due to be opened at the start of the 1965-66 season, was the backdrop; Arsenal were United's opponents. The Highbury side provided strong resistance in what was United's final home match of the season. But after six minutes Law, playing with his knee heavily bandaged to protect the injury sustained against Liverpool, squared the ball to Best. The Irishman snappily opened the scoring with a drive from just inside the penalty area. Law made it two for United on the hour after the ball had rebounded from the bar. And in the final minutes Law hit home Best's corner to make it 3-1.

Law ended the season as top League goalscorer with 28 goals in total. 'I think the word "electric" sums up Denis Law really,' said Bobby Charlton. 'He was so bright and sparks seemed to be flying everywhere whenever he was around and creating problems for defenders. If goalkeepers dropped the ball even six inches he was like greased-lightning and he had it in the back of the net.'

George Best directs the ball towards goal in Manchester United's vital 3-0 victory over Liverpool in April 1965. Tommy Smith of Liverpool appeals for an infringement.

Leeds, United's only remaining challengers, had drawn with Birmingham City in their final game, leaving United above them on goal average. As well as being champions, United were also the best-supported club in England during the 1964-65 season with an average Old Trafford attendance of 46,521. They had the opportunity to end the season two points clear but the new champions lost their final match, going down 2-1 away to Aston Villa on 28 April.

At last, Matt Busby had an opportunity to have another tilt at winning the European Cup. First, the European business of the 1964-65 season had to be concluded. On 12 May, thanks to the FA's permission to play on into an extended season, United were in eastern France, facing Racing Club of Strasbourg in their Fairs Cup quarter-final. Connelly, Herd, Law and Charlton scored the goals in an almost effortless 5-0 victory over an undistinguished French side.

A week later, the two teams played out a nondescript 0-0 draw at Old Trafford. Beforehand, United had been presented with the League Championship trophy. Law, in a separate presentation, was given a trophy to mark his being named as European Footballer of the Year for 1964. That was quite an accolade for a player not involved in that year's European Cup.

On the final day of May, Hungarian side Ferencvaros were at Old Trafford for the first leg of the Fairs Cup semi-final. The Hungarians were led by a future European Footballer of the Year in centre-forward Florian Albert and were a different prospect from Strasbourg. That was emphasized midway through the first half when Tony Dunne brought down Varga on the edge of the United penalty area. Novak's free-kick, aimed with admirable accuracy, whistled through the United defensive wall and past Pat Dunne.

Law equalized with a penalty after Horvath had handled the Scot's header on the line. Then Charlton, showing no lack of appetite for football after nine months of hard running, sent Herd in to score United's second on the hour.

After missiles had been flung on to the pitch from the direction of the Stretford End, Mr Burquet, the Belgian referee, had a warning broadcast to the culprits over the public address system. It was an irritating interruption to an engaging match. With 20 minutes remaining, Charlton stabbed a free-kick forward, Law cut the ball back from the goal-line and Herd swept in United's third. Before the end, however, Rakosi got a second

Tony Dunne (above), John Connelly, Shay Brennan and Bill Foulkes played in all 60 of United's fixtures during the 1964-65 season.

One of Bobby Charlton's many spectacular goals, this time at Blackburn.

for Ferencvaros. That set up an enticing return in the second leg at the Nep Stadium six days later.

The record 70,000 crowd in Budapest saw a less appetising spectacle. There had been one or two niggles in the first match but for the game in Hungary the ball often appeared to be little more than a decoration, a worthless bauble, as far as the players were concerned. Crerand and Orosz of Ferencvaros were sent off for fighting. The only goal came from a penalty, converted for Ferencvaros by Novak after Stiles was ruled to have handled the ball inside the penalty area. It levelled the aggregate score at 3-3. A play-off would decide who would go through to the final. United lost the toss over this so the play-off would take place in Budapest ten days later, on 16 June, nearly two months after the traditional end of the football season in Britain.

United arrived the day before the match after a seven-hour coach journey from Vienna. The British side approached proceedings keen to avoid confrontational incidents. Matt Busby said: 'A lot, of course, depends on the approach of the team to the match. If we play as we can play, and carry the attack, we can win. We made the mistake last time of staying too deep and not coming forward to support the attacks.

'This series is not only a test of reputation and ability, but also of temperament and is an especially good test for us in view of our European Cup commitments next season. But I do not condone rough play. You can ask any of my players what they get from me for that.'

The prize for the winners was a final with Italian side Juventus of Turin. The first match in Hungary had been played in a rainstorm and the mood of the players had matched the weather. This time the sun was out and again the game reflected the conditions.

United showed great composure, defending determinedly and with Charlton and Crerand providing flashes of inspiration, They matched the ball-playing skills of the middle-Europeans, traditionally highly-talented individuals. They are also famous for being able to flight a ball from distance with pace and precision. Shortly before half-time Karaba demonstrated that skill to put Ferencvaros 1-0 ahead.

Ten minutes after half-time, Ferencvaros broke with a swiftness rarely seen in the First Division. The chasing United defence was then turned and put in disarray by Karaba cutting the ball back from the goal-line. The ball fell nicely for Kenyvesi, on his toes just outside the penalty area. His volley shimmered past Pat Dunne to make it 2-0 to the home side. Five minutes from time, Herd scored for United after they had squandered several good chances. It ended 2-1 to Ferencvaros. Again United had gone out to the eventual winners; Ferencvaros went on to beat Juventus 1-0 in Turin in the final. They were also Hungarian champions that year.

Even before that play-off, Matt Busby's words had shown that his thoughts were already on the following season's European Cup, club football's premier prize. It was the one trophy United really wanted. They could now concentrate all their efforts on winning it.

SEASON 1965-66

A week before the 1965-66 League season began, Manchester United and Liverpool played out a 2-2 draw at Old Trafford in the Charity Shield match, raising £13,000 from a 50,000 crowd. The magnificent new cantilevered stand was open and was matched by the quality of the play that could be seen from it and the surrounding viewing areas. Tremendous goals from Best and Herd sent United's fans home happy.

A 1-0 win over Sheffield Wednesday got the League season off to a straightforward start, despite United having to do without Law. He was still troubled by a hip injury received a fortnight previously in a friendly in Nuremberg. At Nottingham Forest in midweek, however, a catastrophic performance by Pat Dunne led to the team being four goals down at one point before eventually losing 4-2.

Dunne was replaced by Gaskell for the next match, a visit to newly-promoted Northampton Town. Although Busby had arrived at something close to a perfect outfield combination, goalkeeper was a position that would prove troublesome for some time. Within weeks, the manager would have recalled Harry Gregg to be his hands-on number one despite the Irishman, still plagued by shoulder trouble, having missed out on the 1964-65 season entirely.

At Northampton, Law, now restored to full fitness, made his first appearance of the season. After taking an early lead through Connelly, United rested on their laurels, eventually conceding an 85th minute equalizer to less skilful but also less complacent opponents.

On 8 September 1965, it was announced that United had made a profit of £48,700 the previous year, the club's highest profit since the 1957-58 season when they had made a profit of £97,957. Wages and bonuses had amounted to £131,000 and gate receipts had increased by £47,000.

As if in celebration, United produced their first away win of the season, at Newcastle, although defensive errors contributed to both of United's goals – scored by Herd and Law. On his 300th League appearance, appropriately in his native north-east, Bobby Charlton's typically enterprising performance was one of the bright spots on an evening when United continued to find it difficult to shake off their early-season sluggishness.

The situation grew in seriousness with a 3-0 defeat at Burnley on a day when United were given the runaround. When they did have possession, United's forwards, perhaps still drunk on the glories of the previous season, showed a tendency to over-indulge themselves. This emphasis on displaying individual brilliance was the antithesis of the teamwork that had brought United the 1964-65 title. Unfortunately, the day was further spoiled by fighting on the terraces – at this time United were followed by an unruly element who had a tendency to cause trouble indiscriminately at both home and away fixtures.

United, with eight goals from eight games, were the second-lowest

George Best, glowering with concentration during a pre-match warm up.

scorers in the League. Drastic measures were taken. For the home game with Chelsea on 18 September, Best was dropped. Another young winger, 18-year-old John Aston, was brought in in his place. Aston had been impressive in the first two games of the season when filling the gap in the forward line that had been left by the absence of the injured Law.

A less eye-catching and more direct winger than Best, Aston created Charlton's equalizer after Venables had opened the scoring for Chelsea. In the second half, a stunning headed hat-trick from Law made it 4-1. Charlton and Crerand had reached perfection in their performances, tearing Chelsea players out of position all over the field.

It was a suitable overture for United's return to the European Cup. The following Wednesday, just over three months after their match with Ferencvaros, United were in Finland to face HJK Helsinki in a preliminary-round European Cup tie. The match, played in the Olympic Stadium, was expected to be an easy one for United. 'I watched the Finns play here a couple of weeks ago,' said Matt Busby. 'They did not impress me then, but I have heard that they can play better if necessary. Therefore we shall not be taking any risks.'

Watched by a crowd of 14,000, many of them Finns supporting Manchester United, the British side opened the scoring after just 30 seconds. Herd got on the end of a move that had been started by 19-year-old John Fitzpatrick, in for the injured Crerand, and carried on by Connelly and Law. After quarter of an hour, Herd drifted out to the wing and crossed for Connelly to nudge home the second.

The amateurs of Helsinki gave United a scare when Pahlman curled a free-kick neatly past Gaskell. Before half-time, though, Law raced on to Connelly's pass to make it 3-1 to United. Law also cleared off the United line before the interval and in the second half a 17-year-old, Peloniemi, got a second for Helsinki. United seemed certain to qualify for the next round but this had been a ragged, unconvincing performance.

Best was back in the United side by the time of the return a fortnight later, at inside-right. Aston remained on the left wing. Connelly headed in the opening goal, off a post, after 13 minutes and from then on United stayed in control of the match. Before half-time Best glided through the HJK defence to make it 2-0. In the second half, Connelly got two more and Best and Charlton one apiece. That gave United a convincing 9-2 aggregate.

Renewed confidence was evident in United's play following that European Cup win. And another mighty clash with Liverpool, in front of 58,000 at Old Trafford, saw United back at their fluent best. Best's pressurizing of Lawrence after 19 minutes gave the Irishman the opportunity to slide in the first goal. Before half-time, Crerand, Charlton and Law combined in a seamless move to make it 2-0. That was also the final score.

On 16 October, the team travelled to London for a League match with Tottenham. At the team's tactics talk, Busby's players presented him with a cut-glass exhibition vase to mark the 20th anniversary of Busby's taking charge as United manager. It was a gesture that moved him greatly and he had to step outside the room and compose himself. The match was also notable for United's first-ever use of a substitute, one Aberdonian, John Fitzpatrick, replacing another, Law, who had picked up a knee injury early in the first half. United played reasonably well, but not like champions, and a 5-1 defeat put a serious dent in their hopes of retaining the title.

At Old Trafford on 6 November, goalkeeper Harry Gregg had an eventful afternoon. He was pelted with stones and bottles from the Blackburn Rovers section of the crowd. Seven minutes from the end, he was sent off after he appeared to have laid out Blackburn centre-half Mike England. A posse of players surrounded the referee in the aftermath of the incident and Gregg took a walk. A dull afternoon was enlivened by three goals after Gregg's sending off. Blackburn equalized from the resultant penalty; Law made it 2-1 with a magnificent effort; then Blackburn equalized through a Crerand own goal. The Blackburn coach was stoned as it left Old Trafford. That match was also notable for George Best having been fielded at outside-right, the start of an extended run for him in that position.

A 5-0 away win at Leicester set United up nicely for a visit to East Berlin and their first-round European Cup tie against East Germany's army side ASK Vorwaerts Berlin. There were 30,000 at the Walter Ulbricht stadium for a match that took place on a Wednesday afternoon. United's players had been unable to train on the pitch, which had been frostbound the previous day. Busby had been moderately impressed when watching Vorwaerts in a previous match but was also confident his forwards would prove superior to the Germans.

The manager's confidence was justified. United turned in a classic performance for an away tie in European competition. Quickly coming to terms with the sub-zero temperature and the bone-hard surface, they smothered Vorwaerts' attacking movements at birth. United saved the cream for the end when they whipped up two late goals. Eighteen minutes from time, Dunne, Best, Law and Herd got together for a move concluded by Law springing into the air to head the opening goal. With ten minutes remaining, Law sent Connelly in for the second. There ended the lesson in goalscoring and, surely, the tie.

Busby said afterwards that he would have been satisfied with a no-score draw but was delighted with the eventual outcome. 'We set out to hold them and come out and play when we could and we did remarkably well.'

Another display of all-round excellence saw United sweep into the quarter-finals after the return match with Vorwaerts. Before half-time, two goals from Herd, fielded at inside-left, from centres by Law, now at inside-right, made the final 45 minutes a formality. Piepenburg scored four minutes from the end to cheers from a Manchester crowd who had begun 'supporting' the Germans in the second half as play slowed considerably. In the final minute, after Law had hit the post, Herd made it 5-1 on aggregate by scoring from the rebound.

Just over a fortnight later, on 18 December, United enjoyed an even more satisfying win. Spurs came to Old Trafford and five goals, sparked off by a stinging 25-yarder from Charlton, gave United a mirror image of the scoreline by which they had gone down at White Hart Lane three months earlier – 5-1. It put United in third place in the League, four points behind leaders Liverpool and with a game in hand.

The new year began with a clash between the two northern rivals. It would go a long way towards deciding which one of them would be that season's champions. A crowd of 54,000 was inside Anfield an hour before kick-off, with thousands more locked out.

It was an unusual day, with United's defence for once outshining the forwards. Gregg enjoyed the better of a personal duel with Liverpool forward St John although he twice needed the help of the crossbar. And Stiles cleared the ball off the line on one occasion even though it had looked as if the ball had gone behind the line before he got to it. Foulkes, Cantwell and Dunne were rock-solid.

United had gone ahead in the second minute, Law gathering a long kick-out from Gregg, galloping clear of Yeats and rounding Lawrence for another great goal. Connelly missed a good chance for a second, shooting against Lawrence then miscontrolling the rebound. Soon afterwards, Liverpool equalized and the score remained 1-1 until two minutes from the end. Then, the merest touch from Milne sent the ball past Gregg for Liverpool's winner.

From then on, it would be all uphill for United in the League in their attempts to catch Liverpool. Their situation was not helped by a series of mediocre results during the rest of January. In their other four League games that month they achieved just one victory and three draws.

By the time Benfica of Lisbon arrived at Old Trafford for the first leg of their European Cup quarter-final on 2 February, United were ready to concentrate all their energies on the European Cup. No British side had won that trophy; indeed, no side from northern Europe had done so. The tournament had been dominated since its inception in 1955 by Benfica, Real Madrid and the two Milan clubs.

Benfica, twice winners of the European Cup and beaten finalists in 1963, and 1965, were led by Eusebio da Silva Ferreira, a forward with wonderful speed and power. The Portuguese club was also one that, like United, had a proud tradition of playing attractive football. Their coach Bela Guttman had, however, said beforehand: 'In these days when everyone is drunk with defensiveness I must drink also.' On that evening at Old Trafford, the potency of United's attacking concoctions was so strong that Benfica were moved to come out of their shells and join in the party.

After five minutes a glancing header from Herd struck the foot of a Benfica post. But on the half hour the 64,000 Old Trafford crowd was stilled. Eusebio gracefully knocked over a corner and Augusto jumped to head Benfica into the lead. Before half-time, United were 2-1 up, Herd then Law finishing off quicksilver moves.

Foulkes and Stiles stood firm as Benfica came looking for the equalizer. On the hour, a free-kick found Foulkes, on this occasion adding his weight to the United attack, and the centre-back dived full-length to head United's third. Ten minutes later, Eusebio crossed for Torres to narrow United's margin of victory to 3-2. It had been an evening of spectacular football, laced throughout with colourful, enterprising attacking from both sides. Eager fans would now have to wait five weeks to see if it could be matched in the return leg in Lisbon.

The Saturday before that match, United went to Wolverhampton for an FA Cup fifth-round tie. The cup was looking increasingly likely to be United's only chance of a domestic trophy after wins in the two previous rounds over Derby County and Rotherham United. Wolves, chasing promotion from the Second Division, were confident of providing an upset in what was the outstanding meeting of that round.

After ten minutes, United were 2-0 down, both Wolves goals having come from penalties. After that, United, with their flawless, tight-knit teamwork, had clamped down hard on Wolves, ensuring that all the good attacking movements would be theirs alone. Law got a goal back midway through the first half, sticking his head forward to convert Crerand's cross into gold. Another Law header, from a Connelly cross, brought United their equalizer before two further goals, from Best and Herd, saw United canter into the quarter-finals.

Benfica looked sure to present a more severe challenge in their Stadium of Light the following Wednesday. They were unbeaten there in all 19 of their previous European Cup ties. They had won 18 and drawn one of those matches, scoring 78 goals and conceding 13. They would have 80,000 fans backing them.

Nevertheless, Busby maintained that United would play to their own strengths and attack the Portuguese from the start. 'It would be foolish to let Benfica get the initiative, especially here,' said the United manager. 'We shall defend when necessary, and attack when we can, for to play defensively would be foolish for us. We shall play to the usual policy which won us the championship last year and we shall have four forwards just when we want them.'

Bobby Charlton was apprehensive beforehand, giving voice to his fears that if United lost out to Benfica it might be some considerable time before they could have another tilt at winning the European Cup.

After six minutes of the match his fears were eased considerably. A free-kick from Dunne on the left wing was angled into the box and Best got the lightest of touches with the top of his head to tip in the opening goal. Other teams might have sat back on such a lead – not United. Six minutes later, Herd did the sensible thing and guided the ball to Best who disposed of three Benfica defenders as easily as brushing some ash off his sleeve before clipping the ball past Costa Pereira. Three minutes later, Herd's pass was taken on by Connelly who made it 3-0.

Before the game, Eusebio had received the trophy awarded to him as the 1965 European Footballer of the Year. He hit the post on the half hour. Half-time came and went with Benfica still subjugated by United but they got a goal back when Shay Brennan put the ball into his own net.

A moment of anguish for John Connelly in United's match with Chelsea at Stamford Bridge in March 1966. Having been presented with an open goal, he watches his header strike a post. Pat Crerand is the other United player looking on.

In the final ten minutes United ensured that the final scoreline would match the grandeur of their performance. Crerand, put in on goal by Law's smooth pass, stretched to reach the ball to turn in United's fourth goal. Then Charlton crept through the heart of the Benfica defence before planting a firm shot in the Benfica net to make it 5-1. Cushions rained down on the Benfica players as the crowd indicated their displeasure at the end of the match in the time-honoured Latin fashion. Some spectators jostled United players as they left the pitch. Nothing, however, could take the edge off an amazing evening.

Afterwards, Matt Busby said it had been United's finest hour. 'And mine too. What else can I say?' he finished.

The following Saturday, 12 March, when United played at Chelsea, 70,000 were inside Stamford Bridge with another 10,000 locked out. It was an anti-climax for United, who performed poorly. Within the opening four minutes of the match, they had lost both of the goals in a 2-0 defeat. It ended any realistic hopes of the championship; United went on to end the season in fourth position, ten points behind champions Liverpool.

Before meeting Partizan Belgrade in the semi-final of the European Cup, United faced Second Division Preston North End in a sixth-round FA Cup tie at Deepdale. Alex Dawson opened the scoring for Preston but

Herd equalized after Law, Charlton and Best had opened up the Preston defence for him. In the replay at Old Trafford, the two sides appeared to be rolling towards another 1-1 draw after Preston had equalized a first-half Law goal. But two goals in the final three minutes from Law and Herd put United in their fifth consecutive semi-final.

In mid-April, Alf Ramsey named his preliminary England squad of 40 for the summer's World Cup tournament. Stiles, Charlton and Connelly were United's representatives. Other than Foulkes and Aston, they were the only English regulars in United's first-team, which was a true British Isles select. Best and Gregg were Northern Ireland internationals while full-backs Brennan and Dunne regularly represented the Republic of Ireland; Crerand, Herd and Law were Scottish internationals.

Foulkes, now aged 34, was rested for United's home League match on 9 April, his place at centre-back taken by Sadler. United fell to their first home defeat since December 1964, Leicester beating them 2-1. Of more consequence to their chances in their two-cup chase was the further damage inflicted on a knee injury that George Best had first suffered at Preston.

The European Cup semi-final that followed on 13 April was a poignant occasion for Busby: it meant a return to Belgrade. United would be playing this important match at the Yugoslav People's Army stadium. This was the very stadium where five of Busby's young hopes had played their final football match eight years previously.

Partizan were on an unusual bonus to win the tie – if they did so, the players would share one-third of the takings at the gate. The Yugoslavs expressed a healthy respect for United and stated that they believed they needed a victory by two goals at home if they were to negotiate successfully the return at Old Trafford.

In front of 55,000 true partisans, United struggled to cope with a team who were tougher than Benfica and who were happy to provide the evidence of it. United had started confidently, Herd shooting just over the bar, Law hitting it with a header. Two minutes after half-time, though, Partizan, who were always quick and sharp, made it 1-0. Hasanagic, their centre-forward, anticipated a cross from Jusufi and headed the ball cleanly past Gregg.

As the game progressed, the tackling became progressively wilder and it

Soskic, the Partizan Belgrade goal-keeper, parries a shot from Denis Law in the 1966 European Cup semi-final at Old Trafford. Law immediately goes on the hunt for the rebound.

was United whose rhythm was upset more than Partizan. With 20 minutes remaining, Partizan got the goal they felt they needed, through a fine piece of Slavonic football craft. Becejac stunned a cross from Mihailovic, shielded the ball in the same movement, then whirled round to crack the ball past Gregg.

The physical contest dominated the rest of the match and bottles were thrown from the crowd. That prompted Partizan goalkeeper Soskic to leave his goal to appeal to his fellow countrymen to cease their antisocial behaviour. The score remained 2-0 to Partizan. They had the result they had wanted before the match. It was as black and white as Partizan's shirts that United were teetering on the brink of European Cup elimination.

United's position was further weakened with the news that Best had severely aggravated his knee injury when stretching for the ball 15 minutes from the end of the match in Belgrade. He would play no further part in United's season and would need a cartilage operation before returning to action at the start of the following season.

Matt Busby accepted that United had been lucky to return to Old Trafford with a second chance and said: 'I think we can give them two goals at Old Trafford and beat them. We must do something, for we really were bad, and the players are sick about all those chances we missed before half-time when I would have given any odds on our victory.'

Having successfully frustrated United the previous week, Partizan set out to do so again at Old Trafford. Defending in depth, they rarely showed any ambition in terms of threatening Gregg's goal. Again, it was a hard, physical match and with the score still 0-0 and United growing increasingly desperate, Crerand and Partizan's outside-left Pirmajer finally declared open warfare on each other. After just seconds, Swiss referee Mr Dienst stopped the bout and dismissed both players.

With 17 minutes remaining, Stiles squeezed a shot past Soskic from an acute angle. Despite further intense United pressure, the Partizan defence held out for the rest of the match. United had failed, by the narrowest margin possible, to become the first British club to reach a European Cup final. Partizan would go on to lose 2-1 to Real Madrid in the 1966 Final in Brussels.

United forwards David Herd (left) and John Connelly (centre) are thwarted by a goal-line clearance in the 1966 European Cup semi-final second leg with Partizan Belgrade at Old Trafford.

Eusebio of Portugal (right) is challenged by Zhechev of Bulgaria during one of the three World Cup matches played at Old Trafford in July 1966. Portugal defeated Bulgaria 3-0 and went on to reach the World Cup semi-final. There they were undone by the running and shooting of Bobby Charlton who scored both goals in England's 2-1 win.

United carried their bruises from that match into the FA Cup semi-final with Everton at Burnden Park, Bolton, three days later. A United side that looked fatigued rarely threatened West in the Everton goal. He had to make just one real save in the entire match. Everton hit a post and Gregg made a fine save from Trebilcock but with just 12 minutes remaining, United looked like holding out for a replay. Then, however, Temple speeded past Brennan and crossed for Harvey to score the goal that sent Everton to Wembley.

Manchester United ended the season without honours but having drawn a great deal of honour, yet again, from the manner in which they had played. The club would maintain those high standards during the following season but in almost every other way it would be entirely different to the season just past.

That summer, Mancunians could watch World Cup action at Old Trafford as it played host to Hungary v Portugal, Bulgaria v Portugal and Bulgaria v Hungary. All three matches drew crowds of fewer than 30,000 but United's involvement was regarded as a success by the World Cup organising committee. Les Olive, secretary at United, commented: 'The clubs that staged the games had the opportunity to improve their facilities. We had grants from the Government, and the Football Association helped out. For instance, we built a railway footbridge at the Stretford End. We also built the new North Stand but didn't get help with that because it was on the drawing board before we knew we were appointed. That might have made a difference in the choice of ground between us and Maine Road.'

SEASON 1966-67

Bobby Charlton and Nobby Stiles had been prominent players in England's 4-2 victory over West Germany in the 1966 World Cup Final at Wembley on 30 July. John Connelly had played in England's first match of the tournament, a 0-0 draw with Uruguay. Those players barely had time to get their breath back before United embarked on a pre-season tour. Less than a fortnight after the World Cup had concluded, United lost 4-1 to both Celtic and Bayern Munich. Then, just a week before the start of the League season, United went down 5-2 to FK Austria Vienna. In that match in Vienna, Stiles showed that his competitive instincts had not been sated by the winning of a World Cup medal. Five minutes from time he was sent off.

Matt Busby admitted he was becoming preoccupied with the heavy leakage of goals. 'Naturally we are concerned but it was not as bad as it seems. We gave away more silly goals than we have ever done in three successive games. Obviously we have got to do something about it this week,' he said on arriving back at Manchester Airport the Sunday before the season began. The manager also confirmed that United had been interested in signing Mike England but were no longer in the market for the player. 'The price Blackburn were asking was much too high,' he said.

Finishing fourth the previous season meant that United would have no European matches to distract them from domestic matters during the 1966-67 season. So they simply rolled up their sleeves and got down to work in the League. West Bromwich Albion again supplied the Old Trafford opposition on the first day of the new season.

Best, restored to full fitness after his cartilage operation, was back on the right wing. Connelly was on the left. Gaskell was back in goal. For the first three matches, John Fitzpatrick filled in for Crerand. Otherwise it was the familiar United line-up of the mid-1960s that took the field.

Before kick-off, both sides formed a guard of honour for Charlton, Stiles and Connelly, in recognition of their achievements with England in the World Cup. Charlton, the 1966 Footballer of the Year, wasted no time in continuing his England form for United. In the opening minute he freed Best to score United's first. Stiles, after eight minutes, hammered the ball into the West Brom net. Law got the third with a powerful header. Herd's 25-yard shot made it four then the same player got United's fifth. In between, West Brom got one back. Only 20 minutes of the match had passed.

United had shown, individually and collectively, that they were anything but a spent attacking force, regardless of their pre-season results. A record win was in sight, but the remaining 70 minutes were less encouraging for United's fans. In the searing summer heat, the players eased off and West Brom exposed some defensive frailties to claw back two more goals.

Prior to the match, plaudits were paid to Jimmy Murphy, Busby's assistant manager, in recognition of his 20 years' service to the club. The Welshman served as the perfect foil to Busby, his outgoing, extrovert nature contrasting with the Scot's more reserved persona. Murphy, on receiving a silver coffee set, coffee table and canteen of cutlery, said: 'United is my whole life and only love.'

In contrast with their opening match, United left it late before picking up the points at Everton the following midweek. Trailing 1-0 with little over 20 minutes remaining, they equalized at high-speed. Best, thinking too quickly for the Everton defence, sent Herd away for a swift cross. Law, matching the crosser's pace, headed the equalizer on the run.

After a series of feuds had threatened to get out of hand, referee Mr Finney got the two captains, Law and Labone, together. They helped calm their colleagues' tempers. The truce looked about to be reflected in the scoreline until, well into the final minute, Charlton's shot was blocked by Everton defenders, the ball fell to Law and he tidied up to give United a satisfying, hard-fought 2-1 win.

A 3-1 defeat at Leeds, distinguished only by the flowing move that led to Best's goal, briefly broke United's stride. 'The thing I disliked most was playing against Leeds,' said Best, 'because they could play and kick, and that combination is dangerous. It was a shame because they were a good side and the lad I usually played against was Paul Reaney, one of the best players I've ever played against. He could play. And I used to hate to admit that I didn't want to play against anybody, but I didn't want to play against Leeds because they were good at what they did.

'But I enjoyed playing against Tottenham, Liverpool and, of course, Manchester City when they were going well. The atmosphere was great and it was a challenge to play against them.'

On 31 August, United completed an early 'double' over Everton, with a 3-0 win at Old Trafford. Urged on throughout by Law, their tireless captain, it was fitting that he should score their final goal. Straining every muscle in his upper body to reach a ball that most forwards would have declared dead, he got to the ball for a scoring header just as it was about to go out of play. It was an inspirational sight, especially as United had already appeared assured of the win. There would be few mutterings of dissent if such a captain were to ask his team-mates to give of their all. Sadly, this was another game in which fighting broke out in the Stretford End.

A 3-2 home win over Newcastle found Law again in indefatigable mood and Best at his best. He utilized his skills for the benefit of the team rather than, as he occasionally did, playing to the gallery.

A setback followed in front of 45,000 at Stoke, the home side outplaying United in a similar fashion to the way in which the Old Trafford side usually overwhelmed other teams. That crushing 3-0 defeat was followed by another one – 2-1 at White Hart Lane to Tottenham on 10 September – that further blighted the good early start to the season. It was a particularly hard defeat for United's players to take – they had been leading 1-0 with five minutes remaining. Foulkes made his 500th League appearance in that game but questions were being raised as to his effectiveness.

United's goal in that game in London had been a real pleasure. Best hooked the ball over his head and high into the air above the six-yard-box. It was a difficult ball for Law to judge. But he positioned himself beautifully and stood almost rooted to the spot before pulling his head back, woodpecker-like, to plant the ball firmly in the top corner of the Spurs net. In the aftermath of that moment, Law had a shot cleared off the line and a Best effort made full contact with a post.

In defence of their defence, United could offer the explanation that

Sadler, helping out at the back, was still suffering from concussion at the time of the goals. Additionally, Gaskell had a foot heavily bandaged to protect a still-tender ankle injury. Yet while Gaskell and Gregg had served the club well, there appeared room for improvement in United's goalkeeping.

A rare excursion into League Cup territory seemed to offer United some respite from the torrid time they were having in the League. It was only their second appearance in the tournament. But without the injured Law and Charlton, who was given a rest, United suffered a third successive battering of their morale. On a miserable night they fell 5-1 to Blackpool, their defence as bedraggled as most of the sodden spectators.

A positive outcome was that United would now face just one more mid-week fixture between mid-September and March with the exception of the traditional Christmas programme. That would allow the players the opportunity for full rest and recuperation between League fixtures.

That week, Busby tackled the team's goalkeeping problem, signing Alex Stepney from Chelsea for £55,000, a record fee for a goalkeeper. He made his debut on 17 September in the home match with Manchester City and would be a constant presence in the United side for the rest of the season. Busby had finally found his exceptional eleven: Stepney, Brennan, Dunne, Crerand, Foulkes, Stiles, Best, Law, Sadler, Charlton, Aston.

In the Manchester derby, a gem of a goal from Law gave United both points against an inferior City side. Law found Aston, ran on to the winger's pass, took the ball round City goalkeeper Dowd

Nobby Stiles patrols the Manchester United goal-line in the local derby with Manchester City in September 1966. Bill Foulkes provides back-up.

and parked it in the net. Admittedly, Law was slightly lucky to be still on the field, having earlier started a scrap with City's Pardoe on the blind side of the referee.

The day before the home match with Burnley on 24 September, John Connelly was transferred to Second Division Blackburn Rovers. Busby was well-served for wingers: in Best he had the trickiest and in Aston one of the fastest in the League.

Best it was whose twisting and turning sparked off a win over Burnley that settled the team after some disturbing results. At the end of another of his special runs he was thumped by a desperate defender but as he fell, rag-doll-like, he still managed to shoot. The ball was half-stopped by the combined efforts of goalkeeper and defender but they only teased the ball into the air. Law met it with the perfect overhead kick for the opening goal. United swept on to a 4-1 victory.

'Football in the '60s was so much fun because you knew when you went out to play against teams that there was going to be lots of excitement,' said Best. 'There were very very rarely 0-0 draws. You knew there were always going to be goals and sometimes goals galore. It was tremendous stuff. We played in the way the game should be played.'

A 4-1 defeat at Nottingham Forest, in the absence of Law, kept United out of touch with the League leaders. Top of the League that first week of October were Chelsea who, in contrast to United, remained unbeaten. Second were Tottenham Hotspur and third Stoke City.

Back in Blackpool for a League match, Busby dropped Foulkes and

Prime time for George Best as he relaxes in October 1966 with then girlfriend Miss UK Jennifer Lowe.

Brennan, bringing in Cantwell at centre-half and 20-year-old Mancunian Bobby Noble at left-back. United won 2-1, leaving them on 14 points, three behind new leaders Tottenham who had 17. Stoke, Leicester and Chelsea were on 16 and Chelsea were the visitors to Old Trafford the following Saturday. Law was back for United and an evenly-balanced match saw Chelsea's defensive organization cancel out United's flair. It ended 1-1.

After a weekend when six United players had been in international action for England, Scotland, Northern Ireland and the Republic of Ireland, United met Arsenal at Old Trafford. An ordinary performance led to a 1-0 win.

Following United's draw with Chelsea three weeks previously, Alan Hardaker, Secretary of the Football League, had written to both clubs commending the high standard of sportsmanship shown by their players. United went south to Stamford Bridge on the first Saturday in November seeking more than compliments.

Law had stubbed his toe in training the previous day and he, along with fellow invalids Cantwell and Dunne, missed the match. Striking wing play saw all three United goals scored by their flank men. For the second United goal, Best used the outside of his left boot to flick the ball past McCreadie, who had sniped unsuccessfully at the Irishman's ankles all afternoon. Best ran on to his own perfectly-weighted ball and, without appearing to adjust himself, slipped the ball into the Chelsea net. The other two United goals were scored by Aston. Keeping United on an even keel amid all the trickery in their 3-1 victory was Pat Crerand, who appeared to have the eyes of a lynx, such was the perspicacity of his passing.

At home to Sheffield Wednesday in mid-November, Law was back in the line-up and Charlton got proceedings off to a flying start with a dramatic 30-yard shot in an accomplished 2-0 win. That win brought United up on the heels of leaders Chelsea, two points behind with a game in hand. It was followed by an all-round exhibition of flowing football in a 2-1 win at Southampton.

After scoring two marvellous goals on that trip to the south coast, Charlton was at centre-forward for the home match with Sunderland. He was upstaged by Herd who scored four goals, even emulating Charlton with his first, a 35-yard stunner. Charlton did hit a post in the 5-0 win but it was Law who got the other United goal. The match was also notable for a mature performance at centre-half by Sadler who showed he had the steadiness required to play in that position.

The final day of November saw United play their game in hand, away to Leicester City. The gates were locked before kick-off with 40,000 inside Filbert Street. Law opened the scoring midway through the first half. When his long-range shot reached the Leicester six-yard-box it whisked across the mud in the goalmouth and past Banks.

A more clean-cut effort followed for United's second, early in the second half. Best dodged past several defenders and, as if tired of their efforts to stop him, ended the sideshow by drawing back his right foot and placing the ball in the top corner of the Leicester net. Friend and foe alike in the crowd acknowledged a goal that transcended the barriers of bias. United ended 2-1 winners. At the end of that 90 minutes, Manchester United were top of the English First Division.

A hiccup followed at Villa Park. United's performance contained all that was wanted by their fans except in terms of their finishing. They created a dozen good chances but took only one of them. Villa made the most of the few opportunities that came their way to win 2-1. United still remained in first position in the League.

Injury and illness kept Law and Stiles out of the home match with Liverpool on 10 December when 62,500 witnessed an enthralling game. It was Best's day, the Irishman rising to the occasion as if determined to single-handedly prove to the reigning champions that he and his team-mates would be worthy successors. A smart, left-footed shot and a penalty that crashed in off the underside of the bar provided the factual evidence of his effectiveness in the 2-2 draw.

Best also made his mark in the referee's book after toppling Yeats, Liverpool's massive centre-half and captain. That would have been a notable achievement for anyone, much less the lightweight Best, who was also half-a-foot shorter than his opponent. United remained on top, with Chelsea second and Liverpool in third place.

Law and Stiles were back for the trip to West Brom on 17 December. By half-time, the fans had seen seven goals and United were leading 4-3. Although contributing to a fantastic afternoon's entertainment, United did ride their luck. Albion had probed for defensive weaknesses and found them. In the second half they twice struck the United woodwork but the scoreline remained unchanged.

On Boxing Day, United suffered an unexpected 2-1 defeat away to Sheffield United. It was to be their final League defeat of the 1966-67 season. The following day, they scrambled to a scrappy 2-0 win over the same team. Both the goals were worth seeing; a 30-yarder from Crerand and a pacy run and shot from Herd. That put United two points clear of Liverpool at the top although the Anfield side had briefly replaced them there after the Boxing Day slip-up.

Before the second match with Sheffield United, it was announced that Bobby Charlton had been voted the 1966 European Footballer of the Year, one vote ahead of Eusebio with Franz Beckenbauer, the German, third in the voting.

The final match of the year was a rugged but entertaining 0-0 draw with Leeds. Stepney was in outstanding form, Leeds hit the woodwork twice and Aston had a header cleared off the Leeds line by Hunter. United went into 1967 as League leaders.

The postponement of United's match with Newcastle saw United leapfrogged at the top by Liverpool. A 1-0 win over Tottenham in mid-January took the standard of football seen at Old Trafford that season to new heights, both sides blending to create high-grade football. The match was settled by an Aston free-kick.

The Manchester derby the following Saturday saw Stiles back after a three-week suspension. Law was missing for a second week through injury. A last-minute equalizer for City after Foulkes had headed in off the cross-bar 15 minutes from the end produced a draw. It was a fair result on a day when both sides' defences were on top form.

A capacity 64,000 crowd, including 21,000 fans from the Potteries, greeted the teams at Old Trafford as United and Stoke City lined up for their third-round FA Cup tie on 28 January. A competent second-half performance saw United into the next round. Their 2-0 win came courtesy of a Law header and a Herd run-and-shot. Crerand, as so often, was outstanding while Foulkes was now enjoying an Indian Summer to his United career.

After a 1-1 draw at Burnley, United were back in second place, a point behind Liverpool and one ahead of Nottingham Forest. Forest, now managed by former United captain Johnny Carey, were United's visitors the following Saturday, 11 February. A crowd of nearly 63,000 were presented with another cornucopia of skills at Old Trafford but with three minutes remaining the match remained deadlocked at 0-0. Then, Forest goalkeeper Grummit made a terrific save to turn the ball behind for a corner. Charlton took the kick. When the ball sailed over Law, sometime opportunist as well as artist, connected with the ball somewhere around his waist to send it over the line for the only goal of the game.

An injury to Foulkes meant he missed United's fourth-round FA Cup tie with Second Division Norwich City on 18 February. It was the first time he had missed an FA Cup match for United after playing in 61 consecutive ties for the club. Despite one of Law's best-ever goals for United, they tumbled to an unexpected 2-1 home defeat. That result meant their minds would be even more focused on the League. United had outclassed Norwich but with Best and Charlton off-form and Norwich defending stoutly the afternoon produced a freak result.

Bobby Charlton scored twice – his first goals for more than three months – in a 4-0 home win over Blackpool on the final Saturday in February. United also regained leadership of the First Division that day, winning it back from Liverpool, who had drawn at Fulham the same afternoon. Had United won by just 1-0, they would have remained in second place, on goal average.

The next fixture for United was a Friday night date with Arsenal. The match, on 3 March, was watched by nearly 64,000 at Highbury and by 28,423 at Old Trafford where this became the first League match ever to be shown on closed-circuit television at Old Trafford. A couple of swerves and a cross from George Best laid on Aston's 54th minute equalizer in a thrilling 1-1 draw that equalled the enthusiasm of the watching throng.

United were the main attraction in the League and the following week there was another massive crowd to see their band of travelling entertainers, this time at St James' Park, Newcastle. Liverpool had briefly knocked United off the top again but while the Manchester club were in the north-east, Liverpool were playing an FA Cup tie at Everton. A 0-0 draw at Newcastle put United back on top, again only on goal average.

A fortnight later, on 25 March, Liverpool would be United's hosts. United teed themselves up for that game with a 5-2 home win over Leicester. Prior to the Leicester match, Charlton was presented with two trophies – one to mark his award as European Footballer of the Year for 1966, the other for being voted best player in the 1966 World Cup. 'Just to be on the same pitch as Bobby was a great pleasure,' said George Best. 'I've never seen anyone go past players as easily as he did. He glided past.'

In a United shirt that 1966-67 season, Charlton had rarely recaptured the form that had inspired England the previous summer. Charlton had, after all, been playing for club and country almost continuously for 18 months. He was back at his best against Leicester, as if receiving those two trophies had reminded him of what he was capable. Apart from scoring United's second goal with an awesome drive, he popped up all over the attacking half of the field, displaying all his old effervescent passing and shooting.

There was also sadness for United in that game. David Herd suffered a broken leg in the opening minute that was to put him out of the side for the rest of the season. Typically, he had done so in the act of scoring United's opening goal.

On the same day, Liverpool lost at Burnley, setting up what should have been an exciting near-climax to the season at Anfield the following Saturday. Instead, the match between Liverpool and United turned out to be an uneventful 0-0 draw. The race for the title remained exciting. Both sides now had nine games remaining. United were two points clear of Liverpool and three ahead of Forest.

An equalizer by Stiles seven minutes from time in a 2-2 draw at Fulham that was watched by 47,000 maintained United's two-point lead. The following evening, when United received Fulham at Old Trafford, a 2-1 United victory resulted from another hugely entertaining match between the two sides. This time United needed a last-minute header from Foulkes to keep them two points clear of their pursuers, now led by Nottingham Forest. United would need all their nerve to hold off the five clubs now in close proximity to them at the top of the League.

In their next League match, on 1 April, United dominated West Ham from start to finish. An intricate intervention from Best created Charlton's opening goal. They were then frustrated by a debatably disallowed goal. A clear penalty was given as a free-kick outside the West Ham box. Then a penalty award was missed by Law five minutes from time. After having taken a third-minute lead, it was three minutes from the end before United added to their tally, Best making it 2-0 then Law making it 3-0.

United stumbled to a 2-2 draw at Sheffield Wednesday on 10 April, squandering a two-goal half-time lead. Both goals had come from Charlton when he finished off sparkling support work, first from Best, then from Dunne and Law.

On 15 April, Denis Law scored the first goal in Scotland's 3-2 win over England at Wembley. That ended the then world champions' 19-match unbeaten run. The following Tuesday, United enjoyed an easy 3-0 win over Southampton through well-taken goals from Charlton, Law and Sadler.

As United close in on their second League title of the 1960s, Nobby Stiles joins the attack during the 3-0 win over Southampton in April 1967.

On 22 April, United went to Sunderland, who had done United a big favour in beating Forest in midweek. That had left United three points clear at the top with four games to go. A dull 0-0 draw was the result at Roker Park but the weekend was brightened by Forest drawing at Arsenal. That kept United firmly on course for the title.

United's penultimate match at Old Trafford that season, on the final Saturday in April, saw them go behind to Aston Villa after 15 minutes. Some moments of magic in the second half brought a nervy win. Best set up Aston who squeezed the ball past several defenders and into the net. Law headed in via the underside of the bar. Best himself went on a bewitching dribble before guiding the ball into the top corner of the Villa net to complete the 3-1 win.

Law had been desperately unlucky to have a second-half goal disallowed for offside. There had been several Villa defenders between him and goal when he received the ball and he was booked for his protestations. He

Denis Law challenges West Ham United goalkeeper Mackleworth during the match at Upton Park in May 1967 that saw United clinch their fifth league title since the Second World War.

had been lucky not to be booked even earlier after looking to pick fights with a number of his opponents. He completed a busy afternoon when, five minutes from time, he untied his boots, put them under his arm and proceeded to finish the game in his stocking soles.

A point in their final away fixture, at West Ham on 6 May, would now be enough to give United the First Division title. They completed their season's work in style.

An hour before kick-off, 38,424 were locked inside Upton Park, creating a postwar record-crowd for a match at that stadium. After two minutes, Charlton pounced to dispossess West Ham right-back Burkett and start the scoring. Three minutes later, Aston crossed for Crerand to get a rare headed goal. In ten minutes, Foulkes tidied up a loose ball to put United 3-0 ahead.

United continued to set West Ham unanswerable questions. Best made it 4-0 before half-time and a Law penalty took the score to 5-1 shortly afterwards. Ten minutes from time, Law sent the ball high into the West Ham net for a glorious sixth. At the end, United fans invaded the pitch and were addressed briefly by Matt Busby.

The following day, he was already looking forward to the 1967-68 season. 'We would obviously like to win the championship again,' he said. 'But we all feel that we must have a real go to win the European Cup. I believe the present team is good enough but obviously if the right player comes on the market we shall buy. I don't think we would have won the championship without Stepney. The First Division is becoming harder to win every season and next year it will be even harder now that Spurs, Nottingham Forest, and Chelsea are all emerging as challengers.

'It was at Easter, when we drew at Liverpool and Fulham that I felt we would win it and it has been very satisfying in the last few weeks to be in a position where we could afford to make a mistake. The cup defeat by Norwich, although a bitter disappointment at the time, proved to be a good thing. With only the League to worry about we have been better equipped both physically and mentally. Ability is no longer enough although there is no substitute for it. You have to have a combination of ability plus work rate.'

Before the final match of the season, at home to Stoke City on 13 May, 61,071 saw United's players receive the championship trophy and winners' medals. The teams played out a relaxed 0-0 draw. United's players did a lap of honour with the trophy. The injured Law missed the game but paraded with his team-mates in a track-suit. Matt Busby joined them. Toilet rolls, a favourite missile of English football fans in the 1960s, flew from the terraces on to the pitch as the fans added to the celebrations. Busby thanked the fans and players for their support throughout the season.

United finished the season four points clear of second-placed Nottingham Forest. United, Liverpool and Arsenal had now all won seven titles each. Six of United's home matches had attracted crowds of over 60,000. The highest attendance was 62,727 for the visit of Nottingham Forest. The lowest was 41,343, the crowd on the opening day of the season against West Brom. Denis Law, with 23 goals, was United's top goalscorer in the League.

Those pre-season results in the late summer of 1966 had been misleading and, after the season's unravellings, they did not look so bad after all. Bayern Munich had gone on to win the European Cup-Winners' Cup. Celtic, 12 days after United's match with Stoke, became Britain's first European Cup winners with a glorious 2-1 victory over Internazionale of Milan in the final in Lisbon. United could now look to that win by Celtic, the team Busby had loved as a boy, for inspiration as they sought to become the first English club to be champions of Europe.

Matt Busby celebrates winning the 1967 League title with his players on the Old Trafford pitch after the final match of the season with Stoke City in May 1967.

Title celebrations in the United dressing-room at Upton Park – Jimmy Murphy is at Matt Busby's shoulder.

SEASON 1967-68

In the summer of 1967, United had gone on the longest tour ever under-taken in the club's history. On 17 May, United played the first match on their itinerary; a 3-1 defeat by Benfica in Los Angeles, California. After another defeat in the USA, 4-2 to Dundee, United moved on to New Zealand and Australia where they were unbeaten. After 12 games in total, mostly against regional selects, United had scored 55 goals and conceded 11. The tour ended in Western Australia on 27 June. Memories of their travels remained fresh as United's players began the 1967-68 season on 12 August.

United had been the first winners of the Charity Shield, in 1908, and they began the 1967-68 season with a stylish performance in the traditional curtain-opener to the season. Cup-winners Tottenham, provided an equal contribution to a riveting match, watched by over 54,000 at Old Trafford. This contest was most notable for one of Spurs' goals in the 3-3 draw being scored from a kickout by their goalkeeper Jennings. Two Charlton shots and a six-yard-special from Law convinced those present that the season ahead was going to be as enjoyable for United as the previous one had been.

Tottenham centre-forward Jimmy Greaves is stopped by Nobby Stiles during the 1967 Charity Shield match.

Brian Kidd, an 18-year-old forward who had been signed while still a Manchester schoolboy, followed his Charity Shield appearance with his League debut at Everton the following Saturday. It was another shaky start to a League season for United who were subdued by Everton's superior all-round play and lost 3-1.

A month later, before their first-round European Cup match with Hibernians Valletta of Malta at Old Trafford, United drew 1-1 at Sheffield Wednesday. A powerful header by Best from Francis Burns' cross saved the day – and a point for United. Eighteen-year-old Glaswegian Burns was another of Busby's schoolboy signings. He had made his debut against West Ham a fortnight earlier and would remain in the left-back position through-out the season. Tony Dunne switched to right-back as Shay Brennan, at 30, became a less regular starter in the first-team. The draw with Wednesday was United's fourth draw in their opening seven games, which had also yielded two wins together with that defeat at Everton. Those results left United comfortably positioned to make a challenge in the League.

Against Hibernians, Kidd's run and cross let Sadler head the ball past Hibernians goalkeeper Mizzi after 12 minutes of the Old Trafford leg of the tie. The Maltese were never likely to offer United any serious danger of elimination but Best, in particular, displayed a tendency to over-elaborate. Too often on the night United appeared content to play with rather than against their opponents.

Shortly before half-time, Law moved proceedings up a gear with an unstoppable 30-yard shot to keep the 43,000 crowd happy. Sadler, at inside-right, made it three with a firm, accurate shot after Best had side-stepped a couple of defenders. Sadler laid the ball off to Law for his second and United's fourth to end the scoring on a night that seemed sure to have taken United further in the European Cup. The proceedings had, however, given little indication of just how far they were likely to progress in that season's tournament.

A more satisfying 90 minutes followed at Old Trafford three days later with an awe-inspiring 3-1 win over Tottenham in the League. Best, Law and Charlton were all operating at maximum efficiency and were quite unstoppable. United then flew to Malta to enjoy the sunshine and what looked an easy passage into the next round of the European Cup.

United were at full-strength in the Empire stadium where an enthusiastic 25,000 crowd watched their second leg against Hibernians on 27 September. Matt Busby made his position clear before the match: 'We are here to win. This is the European Cup and we cannot afford to take chances. We are playing our strongest side.' Hibernians' coach, Father Tagliaferro, a Roman Catholic priest, said: 'There is not much we can do against a team like United. I think we shall just have to defend and do our best.'

On a sand and gravel playing surface, United slipped and stumbled and tumbled into the next round. They never quite mastered the conditions, although Charlton did hit the bar. Early in the match, Best twice juggled the ball past defenders only to slip when preparing to make final contact with the ball. Eventually, United, whose opponents had rarely looked like scoring in either leg, were content to play out a 0-0 draw that took them into the next round.

Again, a more satisfying performance followed United's return to League action. Two first-half goals from Charlton gave them a 2-1 win over Manchester City at Maine Road. Both clubs were challenging at the top of the First Division.

With European football not yet providing any serious distractions, United were fully able to maintain their championship challenge. By the time they visited Liverpool in mid-November, six weeks after the City match, they were a point behind the Anfield side at the top of the League. Indeed, had United not lost their game in hand against Leeds the previous Wednesday they would have been facing Liverpool as League leaders.

Law was in the middle of a six-week suspension, his third such lengthy absence of the 1960s. He and Ian Ure, Arsenal's Scottish centre-half, had been sent off for fighting in United's 1-0 home victory over the London side on 7 October. Stiles was awaiting a cartilage operation. Fitzpatrick came into the team on the right wing; Aston was on the left. Best started the match at inside-right.

Not only did Best take up Law's position on the day, he scored a goal that would have been described as inimitable Law had the Scot scored it. Best seemed indeed to be imitating Law as he appeared to hang in the air like a hawk at the near post to direct Aston's corner netwards after 18 minutes. Five minutes from half-time, Best scored a goal more typical of himself, accelerating on to Crerand's through-ball before stroking it into

George Best (second right) beats Arsenal defenders Frank McLintock (left) and John Radford (right) to the ball, with Pat Crerand offering aerial support. Brian Kidd (extreme left) and Arsenal's George Graham look on.

the net. It was the decisive goal in a 2-1 victory that took United back to the top of the First Division.

'We shall try to play like that on Wednesday,' said Busby after the consummate United performance at Anfield. Wednesday was to be the occasion of another step towards the European Cup. Again United were in Yugoslavia, this time to face FC Sarajevo, in a tie likely to be as complicated as the one against Hibernians had been straightforward.

A six-hour coach journey preceded United's arrival at their hotel in Sarajevo but with 48 hours to go before kick-off it was unlikely to affect their preparation. Sarajevo, in the European Cup for the first time, appeared to have more deep-rooted problems. Lying close to the relegation places in their League, they were struggling to recover from the loss of half their championship-winning team to rival clubs during the close-season.

On their arrival in Sarajevo, United had been welcomed warmly. At the Kosevo stadium, a 90-minute unfriendly interlude butted into what had, until then, been a most pleasant visit for the British club. A 40,000 crowd, another record inspired by a visit of United, looked on as Best was battered black and blue; Kidd and Burns also. Sarajevo showed a certain quickness of thought and bursts of speed on the break but they weren't quite quick enough to break down the United defence. There was one lucky break for United when Musemic seemed to have scored but the Italian referee ruled that the ball had not crossed the line.

Busby had warned his players that they could expect to take some physical punishment in this game. Most of them did but, importantly, they retained their discipline. Both sides showed occasional flashes of skill. But with the Sarajevo defence the best part of their team, the two teams could only produce half-chances. A night of negativity ended 0-0.

Before the return, Sarajevo promised they would attack in an effort to win the tie at Old Trafford on 29 November. It was to be another testing evening for United, in front of more than 62,000 of their fans.

The early part of the game saw United produce numerous scoring opportunities, Kidd seeing one goal attempt hit a post and the other well-saved by goalkeeper Muftic. In 14 minutes, Sarajevo, organized superbly in both games by centre-back Vujovic, finally cracked under the pressure. Best's header was parried by Muftic and Aston, following up, opened the scoring.

After 58 minutes, Vujovic got in the way of a Best shot and watched the ball spin back off a post, along the line and into Muftic's arms. Minutes later, Best stirred the Sarajevo players into action when he appeared to aim a punch at Muftic. Best had taken a pasting from the Sarajevo defenders but his action inspired the most ugly tackle of all when Prijaca took away Best's legs as if he meant to keep them as a souvenir of his visit to Manchester. The Slav was sent off.

In 63 minutes, Best dealt the worst injury of the night to Sarajevo, beating Muftic with a finely-judged shot. The Sarajevo players, outraged at what they believed was an offside goal, surrounded the linesman. He was given police protection before order was temporarily restored.

Sarajevo were a fair side, however, and, in need of goals, they began to expand their ideas in the final 20 minutes. Their captain Fajlagic broke from defence at speed and found Delalic, who netted. Minutes earlier, winger Antic had brought out the best in Stepney. It was all too late for the Yugoslavs. They soon ran out of time. United had won 2-1. They were in the quarter-finals of the European Cup.

United continued to make the running in the League. A masterful 4-0 win over Wolves on Boxing Day, in front of 64,000 at Old Trafford, put them three points clear of Liverpool at the top of the First Division. Manchester City were third, behind Liverpool only on goal average. The FA Cup proved more disappointing, United going out to Spurs in the third round after a replay.

On 24 February, the Saturday before Polish champions Gornik Zabrze visited Old Trafford for their European Cup quarter-final, United defeated Arsenal 2-0 at Highbury. United remained top, three points clear of Leeds, five clear of Liverpool and six ahead of Manchester City. They had managed to win without Charlton, playing in England's 1-1 draw with Scotland at Hampden, although Law was in his usual place in the United forward line.

Gornik had beaten Dinamo Kiev in the previous round. Kiev, in turn, had previously administered the knockout blow to Celtic in the opening round, the fastest-ever dismissal of European champions.

The Poles offered resistance quite as stubbornly as Sarajevo had, with the difference that they usually operated within the rules. Whenever United did manage to penetrate a well-trained Gornik defence their scor-

Sarajevo players protest vigorously that George Best's goal in their European Cup tie at Old Trafford is offside. Best celebrates with Pat Crerand.

ing efforts were, time and time again, repelled by goalkeeper Kostka. In the first half, United won a series of corners; Kostka would spring from his line to punch them clear. Crerand tried an alternative, a tremendous long-range shot; Kostka tipped it over the bar.

With United pulled into sometimes frenzied outright attack, Lubanski reminded them that the Poles were allowed scoring attempts too. Keeping abreast of Musialek's sprint down the left wing, he had the measure of the winger's cross but not of Stepney, who excelled in saving his scoring effort. In the second half, another rare break by the Poles saw another Lubanski shot saved at full-stretch by Stepney.

Best, the exception to most things, was receiving exceptionally tough, and illegal, treatment from his markers on a night when fast, skilful and sporting football predominated. On the hour, he forged the key that unlocked the Gornik defence. Crerand's pass gave him the raw material to work with and Best wriggled his way past three defenders before sending a shot goalwards. Gornik centre-half Florenski could do little with the speeding ball other than knock it into his own net.

Kostka made another outrageous save, this time from Aston, with 15 minutes remaining. And as United's scoring efforts became increasingly more frantic it looked as though they would have to settle for 1-0. However, another touch of the unorthodox brought them a second goal. Jim Ryan, a replacement for the injured Denis Law, sent the ball across the face of goal and Kidd jabbed a heel at it to turn it past Kostka with seconds remaining.

There was one nagging worry for Busby on an otherwise joyful day. Law's knee had become so badly swollen just a few hours before the game that he had been unable even to watch the match from the stand. He would have to see a specialist with regard to the injury.

Sub-zero temperatures and snow was the weather in Poland when United arrived there for the second leg of the tie with Gornik. The match had been switched from the Stadion Gornik to Katowice's massive Stadion Slaski but Busby was not happy with what he saw there 48 hours before kick-off. 'The snow is a shock,' he said. 'I was dreading this. When I was here to watch Gornik play, a few weeks ago, it was dreadful. If conditions are bad, I shall make representations to the referee, Mr Lo Bello. This match is far too important a game for United. We have come here to play football, and after the first great match at Old Trafford we do not want a shambles of a ground to spoil it here.'

The day before the match the pitch was covered in three inches of snow. 'There are patches of ice underneath and it is dangerous,' said Busby. 'Players could so easily break their legs. If the snow is removed the match cannot be played.' The Poles admitted the conditions were not ideal but said that Silesian teams often played in similar circumstances. They also promised to put salt on the surface. Bobby Charlton said: 'Personally I don't want the match off. They are all so important these days and there is obviously a build-up for a big match like this. The players are keyed up. I feel two goals are enough. Few teams can give us that lead and beat us. But I still shudder to think what would happen if we lose it now. The conditions are difficult. It is the fierce cold as much as anything that worries us. You have almost to run with your eyes shut.'

Referee Lo Bello arrived on the overnight sleeper from Vienna and, on the morning of the match, declared the pitch playable. It was still covered in snow at kick-off time. Over 200,000 applications had been made for tickets to this match but only 100,000 spectators could be accommodated inside the stadium.

In the first minute Musialek went clear on Stepney but screwed his shot wide of goal. With snow still falling, the pitch markings soon disappeared but Lo Bello insisted that the match should continue. The conditions created another chance, this time for Gornik's Lubanski, when Stepney's throwout was held up in the snow. But the Pole shot wide.

Few chances did come Gornik's way, as United tackled with swiftness and a sure-footedness that belied the conditions. With 20 minutes remaining, Lubanski did get a goal for Gornik but United successfully negotiated the remaining minutes and the dreadful conditions to move into the semi-finals.

'It was too much of a gamble,' said Busby afterwards. 'It would have been a sad way to have gone out. This is a prize we have been fighting for for years and it would have been terrible if a two-goal lead had been lost under conditions such as they were. I am delighted naturally that we are in the semi-final for the fourth time. I think the whole of England is too and will wish us well.

'It is very gratifying to us to see the youngsters getting such great experience; Sadler, Fitzpatrick and Kidd coming through this tremendous atmosphere. It is so encouraging for the future. This is a more mature side than the one which lost to Partizan two years ago. But it is as well that we remembered that Gornik beat Kiev and Kiev beat Celtic. If we had not remembered that and learned from the match against Partizan we could have been out.

'I feel this is our year. I think things are running for us this time, and I feel happier than on previous occasions when we have got so far. We were the first club to enter the European Cup, because we felt it was a world game. It is the one thing the club wants to win and the one thing I want to win.'

Inside: Derby day in Manchester . . . Q.P.R.

A fortnight after the Gornik match, United took a first-minute lead through Best in the League match with Manchester City at Old Trafford but eventually went down 3-1. That left Leeds, City and United all at the top on 45 points with Leeds first, City second and United third on goal average. All had five games remaining.

A 4-2 away win at Stoke restored United as clear leaders of the First Division before they faced Liverpool at Old Trafford ten days later. It was another setback for United. They looked frail in a 2-1 home defeat. Stiles and Foulkes were missing and in their absence the defence struggled throughout. By the end of the day Leeds had taken their place at the top.

United were looking to win the English First Division for a record eighth time but in a 1-0 win over Sheffield United the United defence again looked lightweight. That win however, meant United were back on top of the table. With three games remaining, they were the best placed of the top four – themselves, Leeds, City and Liverpool – to win the title. United were also top in terms of sheer popularity – the club's average attendance in the 1967-68 season was 57,522, the highest ever achieved by any English club in the twentieth century. Between 1966-67 and 1969-70 they were the best-supported club in Britain.

The League was temporarily forgotten as United prepared for the Real thing – the visit of Madrid's all-whites in the semi-final of the European Cup on 24 April. Real had won the Spanish championship the previous weekend. They had, by then, also been six-times European Cup winners, eight-times finalists and had competed in every European Cup since the competition had been inaugurated in 1955. Real had, more than any other club, captured the imaginations of people across Europe, showing that wonderful skills and entertainment could be allied to winning.

It was United, however, who showed how to attack in the first leg at Old Trafford. After just three minutes, amid heavy United pressure, Law,

United's patron saint of lost causes, got to the ball just as it was about to go over the goal-line. His cut-back went to Crerand whose shot smacked off the foot of a Madrid post.

Real, despite occasional glimpses of guile, were unable to show off their own skills as United kept them penned in their own half. In 36 minutes, Aston got past Real full-back Gonzalez at the second attempt and squirted the ball back to Best who had ambled into space just inside the penalty area. The winger elegantly found the roof of the Real net with a left-footed shot. United were ahead and looking good to add to their opener.

The 63,200 saw United hit the type of form that had been missing from their League games for weeks. It was as if they were lifted by the occasion and the pursuit of the one trophy they cherished above all others. Numerous chances, almost all of them to United, came and went in the second half but United could not add to their score. It had been a marvellous spectacle, a game that had enhanced the reputations of two of the world's greatest clubs. But United fans wondered whether their side's lead was too slender, too fragile to withstand the rigid examination due at Real's Bernabeu stadium three weeks later.

There was little encouragement for them five days afterwards as United went down 6-3 in an away match at West Brom, with the defence in shreds by the end of the game. On the same night, Manchester City, with a 2-0 home win over Everton, went top of the First Division for the first time in the 1967-68 season. United's 6-0 win over Newcastle on the penultimate Saturday of the season gave them their biggest victory of the campaign but kept them behind City on goal average with one game to play. Best, with a hat-trick, had been outstanding.

On the final, dramatic day of the season, United, watched by 62,471, slumped to a 2-1 home defeat to Sunderland. City won 4-3 at Newcastle. Matt Busby was quick to congratulate his cross-town rivals. United now had to lift themselves for the trip to Madrid and the second leg of their European Cup semi-final with Real four days later.

On the Manchester club's arrival in the Spanish capital, Real's president Santiago Bernabeu spoke with a dignity that befitted his club: 'I want Manchester United greeted and treated and respected as the greatest club in the world. And as our friends for many years nothing must go wrong. If we are beaten in the European Cup by Manchester United on Wednesday then we shall have lost to a great team. We have met them on many occasions and it is about time their luck changed.'

Busby regarded the opening 20 minutes as being hugely important: 'That is the crucial period of the game. In the past we have found that if opposition like this gets a goal then the world goes mad and the players become giants. We must try to contain them for that space of time.

'At the ground on Monday, Bobby Charlton voiced the opinion of all the players that the League was now something of the past. The European Cup was something to go for. Rather than being bad for us to lose the championship, I think it has done us good. That slip in the League could be the spur and the players were all of that opinion both when we trained and when we discussed this European Cup match. This cup Manchester United wants to win most of all. It is and has been uppermost in our minds.'

Law had made the first leg but was now feeling pain in his knee every time he kicked a ball. He was missing from the United team who walked out on to the lush green turf at the Bernabeu in front of 125,000 Spanish fans who had grown anything but complacent with success.

Amancio, regarded by Real as the successor to Di Stefano, was in the home side's line-up after having been suspended for the first leg. He would do much to ensure that this was another sublime example of European competition, the type of match visionaries such as Gabriel Hanot and Busby had hoped for at the birth of the European Cup in the mid-1950s.

After ten minutes, Amancio met Perez' corner with his head – Stepney turned the ball on to the bar. Then Crerand swerved a free-kick just wide of the Real post. In 32 minutes, Real drew level on aggregate. Amancio floated the ball into the United penalty area where Pirri headed past Stepney. Three minutes before half-time, a goal from 34-year-old winger Francisco 'Paco' Gento, who had played in every European Cup tournament since 1955, appeared to put Real in control. A minute later Real's Zoco, in attempting to deal with a cross from Dunne, put through his own goal.

With seconds of the first half remaining, Amancio delivered a powerful blow to United's collective solar plexus. Showing exquisite balance, he took delivery of a pass and, without pausing, struck the ball on the half-volley round several United defenders and into the corner of Stepney's net.

In Real's backyard, United looked cornered. But in the second half they forced Real on to the back foot. Save after save was produced by goalkeeper Betancourt until, with just 15 minutes remaining, United equalized on aggregate for a second time. Crerand's free-kick was headed on by Best and as the ball looped down Sadler met it to finally beat Real's creditworthy goalkeeper. Four minutes later, the unlikely figure of Foulkes shocked both Real and his team-mates by getting forward to take a pass from Best and sidefoot the ball past Betancourt. Ten tense minutes ticked away. Then at last, after four European Cup semi-finals, United were in the final itself. Busby described it as the greatest night in the club's history.

In the final, scheduled for Wembley stadium on 29 May, their opponents would be Benfica who had defeated Juventus, the Italian champions, 3-0 on aggregate in the other semi-final.

In the days leading up to the final, Best was named as Footballer of the Year by England's football writers, at 21 the youngest-ever recipient of the award. Busby was named Manager of the Year.

Five days before United and Benfica met at Wembley, Denis Law went into hospital for a knee operation. 'He will certainly not be able to go to London for the European Cup final,' said Busby. 'The x-rays have shown a shadow on the knee which may be a foreign body from an earlier cartilage operation. The operation will be exploratory and we hope that this will enable Denis to get right.'

Six of the Benfica side had faced England in the World Cup semi-final at Wembley two years previously. Stiles would mark Eusebio, as he had done in that game. Benfica had also played at Wembley before, in a European Cup final. In 1963, they had lost there to Milan three days before United had played Leicester in the FA Cup final.

Both sides' first-choice colours were an almost identical red top and white shorts. So United were to wear all-blue in the final; Benfica would take the field in all-white.

'It is something I have been looking forward to for years,' said Busby. 'I feel confident that we can pull it off and make it the happiest night of my life. It would make up for that terrible disappointment when we lost to Partizan two years ago.'

The 100,000 tickets for the final had been sold even before the finalists were known. Both sides had limbered up on the Wembley pitch the day before; United were supervised by a Busby who looked cool in shades to combat the late-May sunshine.

For the final, Busby had opted to go with the experienced Brennan at right-back. That meant Dunne switching from that position, which he had occupied for most of the season, to left-back. Young Burns, who had been

(top) Bobby Charlton and Benfica captain Mario Coluna exchange hand-shakes and pennants before the 1968 European Cup Final.

almost ever-present at left-back, missed out. Sadler, who had played well in five different positions that season, filled in for Law at inside-left. The United side for their fifth Wembley appearance and first European Cup final was: Stepney, Brennan, Dunne, Crerand, Foulkes, Stiles, Best, Kidd, Charlton, Sadler, Aston.

From the start, on that warm evening, the tackling emphasized the amount at stake. Best was felled frequently by Cruz and Humberto. That restricted his effectiveness in the early part of the match. But over on the left wing John Aston was showing some exquisite touches. With both sides wary of the potency of each other's for-

(centre) George Best speeds past Benfica midfielder Jacinto in the European Cup final at Wembley.

(right) Brian Kidd wins the ball in the air during the early stages of the final with Benfica.

wards, much of the first half was played in a cagey, careful manner. That didn't prevent Eusebio dropping off to an inside-right position in 11 minutes, taking a pass from Torres, eluding Stiles and Foulkes and aiming a shot at goal that struck Stepney's crossbar. Then a Eusebio free-kick was deflected off United's defensive wall and Stepney had to work hard to get to it. United's best chance of the first half came through a Kidd-Sadler one-two but Sadler put the ball wide of goal.

United flew at Benfica from the start of the second half. Aston twice went close to scoring. Eight minutes after half-time, Sadler, on the edge of the penalty area, lifted the

(top) United fans at the European Cup final.

(centre) Bobby Charlton takes control of the ball in midfield during the European Cup final.

(left) In extra-time, Charlton flights the ball over the head of Benfica goalkeeper Henrique for the final goal in United's 4-1 victory.

*Shay Brennan (left)
and Bobby
Charlton (right)
parade the
European Cup at
Wembley.*

*Two days after the
European Cup
final, Matt Busby
shows the captured
trophy to the people
of Manchester.*

ball into the centre of the box in anticipation of Charlton's run. His only option was to meet it with his head and he did so perfectly, giving the ball the gentlest of nudges to send it well wide of Henrique and into the Benfica net. It was a wonderful goal, especially as Charlton rarely scored with his head. Best almost made it two, breaking clear only to be halted by goalkeeper Henrique's dash to clear from well outside his penalty area. Henrique also made a tremendous double save from Best and Sadler.

With nine of the 90 minutes remaining, Benfica's Augusto crossed and Torres nodded the ball to Graca. With United defenders watching Eusebio, Graca was unmarked as he nicked the ball into goal from the edge of the six-yard box with a masterful display of balance and control. In his excitement the scorer leapt to hug one of the photographers behind the United goal. Twice before the 90 minutes were up, Stepney made crucial stops from Eusebio when the Portuguese, now well on top, seemed set to score the winner. 'I had come out too far and I was trying to get back when he shot,' said Stepney of the more clear-cut of Eusebio's chances. 'Fortunately he hit the ball straight at me.' Eusebio had also gone for power rather than precision and had shot with his left rather than his stronger right foot. Those three split-second errors saved United.

It had been a punishing 90 minutes and extra-time looked sure to be draining. 'Had normal time gone on another ten minutes,' said Stiles afterwards, 'they might well have beaten us, but extra-time gave us the chance to pull ourselves together and really show what we could do.'

In the 93rd minute, Stepney's long kick was headed on by Kidd who found Best. The winger went past Jacinto, sent Henrique the wrong way then rounded him before passing the ball into the net with the inside of his left foot. 'It was like something from Roy of the Rovers,' said Best. Two minutes on, Charlton's corner-kick was headed on by Sadler and Kidd helped the ball towards goal with his head. It was half-stopped by the excellent Henrique and when the ball flew into the air Kidd, celebrating his 19th birthday, nodded the ball over the goalkeeper for the third. In the 100th minute, Kidd turned supplier again, crossing for Charlton who remembered Jimmy Murphy's coaching and executed a darting run towards the near post. The forward met the ball at speed but exerted instantaneous control over it to spin it, first-time, high over Henrique's head to make it 4-1. It was a goal that only one of the supreme exponents of the game could have scored. Some photographers were on the pitch as Charlton celebrated with Best. They knew it was all over.

It was the end of a marathon pursuit for Busby. 'I have chased and chased this European Cup with many disappointments but here it is at last,' he said. 'I am the proudest man in England tonight. The boys have done us proud. They showed in Madrid that they have the heart to fight back and tonight they showed us the stuff that Manchester United are made of. I am proud of them all.'

It would be difficult for Manchester United to equal their European efforts of that season. The club's final full season of the 1960s, however, would see Busby ending it the following May again speaking eloquently of his pride at the magnificent efforts of his men against continental opposition.

SEASON 1968-69

Exotic international matches again overshadowed United's domestic season in 1968-69, which proved a disappointing one. By mid-September 1968, they were stuck firmly in the middle of the First Division table, five points behind leaders Leeds United and six above bottom club Queens Park Rangers. In the League they had won four, drawn four and lost two of their matches. United had more important things in mind, namely the World Clubs Cup and a match with Estudiantes of Argentina. All connected with United had started anticipating and savouring this match even as the European Cup-winning celebrations were taking place.

The World Clubs Cup had first been played for in 1960. It was a play-off between the European Cup winners and the winners of the Copa Libertadores, the South American equivalent of the European Cup. Played on a home-and-away basis, in the eight years before United took part it had drawn massive crowds to each of the ties in South America and in Europe.

Until 1967, the matches had seen Latin winners of the European Cup taking on clubs in Latin America. The year before United played Estudiantes, however, Celtic had played Racing Club of Argentina. The Celtic players had suffered provocation of a sort they had never experienced before while the Argentinians disliked the full-blooded tackling of their British opponents. In a play-off in Montevideo, Uruguay six players were sent off – two Argentinians and four Scots – after Celtic's patience finally snapped. Despite those scenes, faith remained in the competition as the ultimate decider as to which club could justifiably claim to be the greatest in the world that year.

As with Celtic the previous year, the Argentinians were immensely gracious towards United on their arrival in Buenos Aires. At their headquarters, United's players were told by the Old Trafford club's staff not to eat salads, drink tapwater or eat bread. They could have toast and approved bottled mineral water.

There was an ominous tone to the pre-match comments from representatives of both sides. On the weekend before the match, Osvaldo Zubeldia, manager of Estudiantes, said: 'In my opinion, these are the two best teams in the world meeting. But anything can happen. There are differences between English and Argentinian football, but they are basically not so different as to provoke rough play. The referee has the responsibility to cope with that problem. This is not a national war. There will be no heroes.'

Sir Matt Busby – he had been knighted for services to football in the summer of 1968 – said: 'It is so difficult for any manager to ensure there is no hot-headedness and that players do not retaliate. You can do all the talking in the world. You can advise in every way. But somebody on the field will be provoked and do something they really do not want to do, and are sorry for it afterwards. But there it is. If you start bickering and carrying on, you do not play at all. You lose your skill, you lose your heads, you lose the match.

'So much depends on the referee. If he shows at the start that he will stand no nonsense, then it must have a beneficial effect. There are differences in interpretations of the rules. Here there is shirt-tugging and deliberate obstruction; our tackling is too strong. It will go on until there is a common denominator. But this is a world game. You cannot run away if there is trouble, and we have been leaning towards each other now for the past two years. We have picked up something from them and they from us.'

Estudiantes, from La Plata, 30 miles outside Buenos Aires, chose to use Boca Juniors' stadium in the Argentinian capital for the match. They were on £1,750 to win the World Clubs Cup. There were over 2000 police on duty on the day of the game and they ensured that misbehaviour in the 85,000-strong crowd was non-existent.

On a hard, bumpy surface, it was difficult to play football. The Argentinians barely bothered trying. Instead, they gouged eyes, delivered sly punches, spat, elbowed and hacked United. Stiles, who had been demonized in the local press during the build-up to the game, came in for particularly tough treatment. Ten minutes from time, he was sent off for disputing one of many debatable decisions by Esteban Marino, the Uruguayan linesman.

Estudiantes had started positively; Bilardo, Suarez and Togneri all going close to scoring in the early stages. Charlton cleared Pachome's shot off the line. After 29 minutes, Togneri opened the scoring, heading Ribaudo's corner past Stepney although Foulkes, in going for the ball, appeared to have been impeded by Conigliaro. Stiles had needed stitches in an eye wound. Charlton required stitches in a leg wound. Best and Burns had been flattened by off-the-ball fouls. It ended 1-0 to Estudiantes, suiting United, who were confident of overturning it at Old Trafford.

Afterwards, Busby said: 'It was disgraceful. If you held the ball you were in danger of your life.

'Is it all worth it? I think we must keep on trying, especially to educate these people to our way of thinking.'

Sir Stanley Rous, the English President of FIFA, who attended the match, said: 'The outstanding feature of it all was the tolerance of Manchester United. We can all be proud of them.'

The Saturday before the return, an injury-weakened United side lost 2-0 to Liverpool to go ten points behind leaders Leeds and just four points off the bottom spot. Already the title looked beyond them. The following day, Zubeldia refereed a match between his Estudiantes players and a team from the Manchester Institute of Science and Technology. At half-time, with his side leading 5-0, he stopped the match because of heavy rain.

A crowd of 63,400, paying record receipts for Old Trafford of £25,000, assembled for the return with Estudiantes on 16 October. 'We've got to attack – if they'll let us,' said Bobby Charlton. 'We're a goal down and defence is no use. And Estudiantes are good players, let no one think otherwise. United try to force backs and half-backs into mistakes. But these chaps give nothing away. They don't make mistakes.'

Estudiantes, masters of gamesmanship, moderated their style for the return. This time, they played right on the border of the rules. After five minutes, Madero's free-kick found Veron at Stepney's left-hand post and he headed the ball across the goalkeeper for the opener. Close to half-time, Crerand set up Law at close-range but the forward lost the ball under goalkeeper Poletti's challenge. Poletti's studs had sliced into Law's leg. The Scot left the field for four stitches and did not reappear.

At one stage, Best had appeared to aim a blow at Estudiantes right-back Malbernat. And in the closing minutes of the match, Best made contact with a punch at Estudiantes centre-back Medina. Both Best and Medina were sent off. As they left the field, Medina had to be restrained by a linesman – he wanted to continue the fight with Best.

Winger Willie Morgan, a £100,000 summer signing from Burnley, drove home a goal for United to make it 1-1. That was how it stayed. Estudiantes had won the World Clubs Cup but their behaviour had greatly devalued the prize.

United still had the European Cup to defend but they continued to struggle badly in the League. Between mid-October and mid-January they won just three League matches. They plummeted to sixth-bottom of the First Division. The European Cup-holders were in serious danger of relegation. Rumours began to circulate that Sir Matt Busby was on the verge of resignation. On 14 January, four months before his 60th birthday, those rumours were confirmed.

At a press conference held in the players' lounge at Old Trafford, United secretary Les Olive read the statement that signalled the end of one of the most remarkable managerships the football world has ever seen. 'Sir Matt has informed the board that he wishes to relinquish the position of team manager at the end of the present season. The chairman and directors have tried to persuade him to carry on and it was only with great reluctance that his request has been accepted. The board fully appreciate the reasons for his decision and it was unanimously agreed that he be appointed general manager of the club which Sir Matt is very happy to accept. The position of team manager will be advertised at a later date.'

Busby said his resignation had nothing to do with the club's League position: 'It would not have made any difference. It is only right my successor should be ready to start at the beginning of a new season. I shall stay in my present capacity until the end of the season and help in any way I can, but I shall not interfere, just as nobody has ever interfered while I have been team manager. And don't worry about United's position. These things happen to everybody and we'll get over it.'

Despite United's downward spiral in the League, they were defending the European Cup in fine fashion. At the time of his announcement they were looking forward to a quarter-final with Austrian champions Rapid Vienna. To get there, United had beaten Irish champions Waterford on a 10-2 aggregate in the first round, Law scoring seven of the ten goals. In the second round, in front of 51,000 at Old Trafford, United faced Belgian champions Anderlecht. In United's first-ever competitive European match at Old Trafford, in September 1956, they had beaten Anderlecht 10-0. It had been United's record victory. This game would be very different.

Early on, Devrindt's shot struck Stepney's boot and span past the post. Then Law missed a penalty which was saved by goalkeeper Trappeniers. In a pulse-quickening game, Puis hit the United post and at half-time the score was 0-0. In 51 minutes, Ryan crossed and Kidd headed in the opener. Twenty minutes later Charlton performed the same service for Law. With 12 minutes remaining, Law made it 3-0 to United. At the end, the United players applauded the impressive Anderlecht team off the pitch. The tie looked as good as over. It was not.

United did take the lead in front of 40,000 at the Parc Astrid where Stiles was booed from start to finish, as he was wherever he went. Crerand

Willie Morgan, a winger, was Busby's first major signing after the European Cup triumph. Here he faces West Ham in September 1968.

found 20-year-old Italian-born midfielder Carlo Sartori with a throw-in and the youngster placed the ball past Trappeniers. By the 70th minute, however, Anderlecht, often attacking with eight men at a time, had scored three goals. But they couldn't get the fourth that would have given them a play-off. Again United applauded their outstanding opponents from the pitch.

The quarter-final with Vienna found George Best, who had been voted European Footballer of the Year in 1968, in brilliant form. He had missed the Anderlecht tie due to suspension following his sending-off against Estudiantes but made up for it against the Viennese in the first leg at Old Trafford on 26 February.

With 63,000 fans looking on, United went all out to finish the tie in the first leg. Best and Charlton were clearly fouled inside the penalty area during the first half but the Yugoslavian referee, struggling to keep up with play, failed to give a penalty on either occasion. Two minutes from half-time, Rapid right-back Gebhardt wilted under pressure after a double one-two involving Best and Law. The defender sent the ball against his own post and the ball trundled towards the goal-line from where Morgan cut it back. It was cleared again, as far as Best, who coolly speared the ball past five Rapid defenders for the first goal. Midway through the second half, Kidd's clever lay-off gave Morgan the second.

With 20 minutes remaining, Best got a goal to match his performance on the night. Another sophisticated one-two, this time with Stiles, brought Best racing into the Rapid penalty area. There he rode three close challenges before toe-ending the ball high into the Rapid net as he was tumbling backwards. A 0-0 draw in Vienna a week later put United into the semi-finals where they would meet Milan, the Italian champions.

The match in Milan would take place on 23 April, four days after United had beaten Burnley 2-0 in the League. They were not scheduled to play another domestic match until 17 May, when they would meet

Action from United's run to the 1968-69 European Cup semi-final. Law scores United's second goal in the 3-0 win over Anderlecht at Old Trafford (below). Best opens the scoring in the 3-0 win over Rapid Vienna in the quarter-final (below right). Morgan watches his shot settle in the net for the second goal in that match with Vienna at Old Trafford (bottom).

Leicester, two days after the return with Milan. That was thanks to the FA specially extending the season in the light of United's European commitments.

In that match with Leicester, United would beat the cup-finalists 3-2 at Old

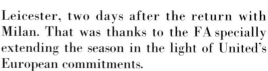

Trafford. That meant United finished 11th in the First Division. They had enjoyed a run of five wins in their final seven matches. United had gone out of the FA Cup in the sixth round, beaten 1-0 at Old Trafford by Everton.

Before the first leg in Milan, Busby said: 'They are a highly professional side. Everybody knows what jobs they have to do and they do it. They are professional rather than ultra-clever players and compare well with Gornik, Benfica and Real Madrid. The biggest menaces to us in attack tomorrow night will be Prati, Sormani and Rivera. I am glad we are playing the first leg away from Old Trafford. I would like to come away from San Siro winning, but if we do come away with the same result as Celtic I shall be very happy indeed.' Celtic had drawn the first leg of their quarter-final in Milan 0-0 but had lost the second leg 1-0 to a Prati goal.

Jimmy Rimmer, a 21-year-old goalkeeper, had made only five first-team appearances before the match in Milan. He made his European debut when he replaced the off-form Stepney for the match in the San Siro. The game was watched by an 80,000 crowd.

From start to finish the Italians controlled the match with their precision play. Rimmer made two fine saves from Sormani and Prati early on, diverting the ball past a post on each occasion. The German Schnellinger opened a way through for Hamrin but Rimmer sped out to thwart the Swede.

After 34 minutes, Milan's pressure finally told. Stiles attempted a clearance but instead ballooned the ball high in the air. As the ball dropped, Sormani and Foulkes challenged each other. The ball flew off their heads and back into the air above them. When it dropped again, Foulkes nudged it away from Sormani with his head but as Crerand swang at the ball with his right foot he mistimed his clearance. The ball rebounded off his back and Sormani pounced to lash the ball past Rimmer from the edge of the penalty area. Shortly after half-time, Sormani missed an open goal but in the 50th minute Milan made it 2-0. Fogli gracefully flicked the ball over Stiles' head and crossed from the right wing. Prati executed the cleverest of dummies and Hamrin was free to prod the ball past Rimmer from the edge of the six-yard box.

United's best effort at getting a goal back came when Kidd's well-struck shot made Milan goalkeeper Cudicini work for his money. But an unhappy night was made even unhappier with ten minutes remaining. Fitzpatrick kicked Hamrin off the ball. A linesman spotted his offence and the United man was sent off.

Busby said: 'We are not beaten yet. We never give up when we have a chance. If we can score one at Old Trafford that will worry them and a second will earn us a replay.'

The three-week gap between the two legs of the European Cup semi-final allowed Busby to give his players a week's break after the first leg. They were then back in full training and travelled to Ireland for warm-up matches in Waterford and Dublin.

Before the second leg with Milan, Nereo Rocco, the Italian side's coach and tactical maestro, said: 'When we played against Celtic in Glasgow, we went out with nothing to lose, and hoping for a miracle. The match against Manchester United is very different. The Italians and the Italian press expect us to win. And if we resist for 20 minutes at Old Trafford, you will see a great Milan.'

On the night, Milan made a good job of smothering United's scoring efforts but they were never able to stifle United's spirit. In the first half, Sormani and Prati, on separate occasions, almost finished the tie when they broke from defence with whippet-like speed. And there was an alarming incident for United just after half-time. Cudicini dropped to the ground, having been struck by a missile from the Stretford End. Referee Mr Machin of France warned the crowd as to their future conduct. Cudicini continued.

With 20 minutes remaining, United at last made the breakthrough. Some loose-limbed twists from Best saw him drift away from three Milan defenders and ease the ball on to Charlton. The centre-forward attacked the ball on the edge of the six-yard box to beat Cudicini with a smart angled shot. United now began to harass Milan intensely. Minutes after Charlton's goal, Crerand shot and Milan defender Santin struggled to knock the ball away from the goal-line. Law, following up, claimed the ball had crossed the line but Mr Machin waved play on. 'The ball was in,' said Law. 'If that had been given we'd have gone on to beat Milan and we would have gone on to win the European Cup.'

Milan hung on to go through on a 2-1 aggregate. As they celebrated in the centre circle, United players lined up to applaud them off the pitch. 'I was delighted with the performance of my team,' said Sir Matt. 'They were magnificent and gave everything they had to pull the game around. Perhaps we had one or two chances we did not take, and you have to accept these when playing against a team which has such a capable defence as Milan has.'

'We felt that we had already played two finals, against Manchester United and Celtic, two excellent teams,' said Milan's 'golden boy' Gianni Rivera. Milan went on to defeat Ajax Amsterdam 4-1 in the final in Madrid with Prati getting a hat-trick.

For United, the following season would be about graft rather than glamour. After two seasons of continuous competition in Europe, the players would have to concentrate on domestic issues. United appeared to have played above themselves during their European run. The following season would go a long way towards establishing how far that was true.

Sir Matt Busby communicates with the crowd after relinquishing the post of team manager. It is 17 May 1969 and United have just completed their season with a 3-2 home win over Leicester City.

SEASON 1969-70

Johnny Carey, the captain of Manchester United when they won the FA Cup in 1948, was one of the most admired managers in the English game during the 1960s. In March 1967, while manager of Nottingham Forest, he was asked by David Lacey of The Guardian about the possibility of Carey succeeding Matt Busby. 'I think no one would ever want to see Matt leave Old Trafford or assume any position other than manager,' said Carey. 'I certainly think he can go on for a very long time and I hope he does. It will be a very unenviable job for the man who takes his place.'

In January 1969, just days before Busby announced his retirement, Carey had gone to Blackburn Rovers as manager. Among others who had been regarded as possible successors were Brian Clough, manager of Derby County, Noel Cantwell, manager of Coventry City, Jack Crompton, the senior trainer at Old Trafford, and Wilf McGuinness, the youth team manager.

Busby had said United were looking for 'someone in his early thirties or older, but no more than 45. He must be experienced because we are not in a position to experiment. He must have already proved himself as a leader who commands respect and he must never make a promise without being able to keep it.'

Wilf McGuinness who took over the coaching and selection of the Manchester United first-team in June 1969.

McGuinness was the man chosen. A Mancunian by birth, in the early 1950s he had been captain of England Schoolboys and had turned professional with United in November 1954. In December 1959, he suffered the broken leg that was to end his career at the age of 22. He remained at Old Trafford where, in 1961, he took up the position of youth team trainer, successfully bringing through a flow of young talent throughout the 1960s. He had also been trainer to the England youth team since 1963 and had been one of Alf Ramsey's four coaches at the 1966 World Cup.

In April 1969, his appointment as chief coach, not manager, was announced. He was 31 years old and had a three-year contract. Busby had strongly wished to keep the appointment in-house to preserve the family spirit at Old Trafford. He would continue to oversee matters as general manager. Busby, after more than 40 years in the game, would be there to offer valuable advice to the coach whenever it was required. McGuinness would work with players on a daily basis and pick the team on a Saturday. It was the type of system favoured by continental clubs.

But as Carey had suggested, as long as Sir Matt remained at Old

Trafford it would be difficult for anyone to regard him in any other light than as manager. The postwar rebuilding of Old Trafford had happened in tandem with his years in charge – he was, literally, in with the bricks.

Although McGuinness had been appointed in the spring he did not take responsibility for the team until 1 June 1969. Any new manager would have found it difficult to step out of Busby's shadow. However, a bit more wisdom on McGuinness' part might have allowed him to enjoy Busby's wisdom to his best advantage. A hearty, outgoing type, McGuinness, still very young, did not help himself by remaining to a large extent one of the lads. He would indulge in such activities as card games on the bus to and from matches.

United lost three and drew one of their opening four League matches in August. Foulkes had struggled badly, so Ian Ure, Arsenal's centre-half, was signed for £80,000. McGuinness had needed a centre-half and Busby remembered the Arsenal man's impressive displays from several games against United in previous years.

In August 1969 Ian Ure, the Arsenal centre-half, became the first major signing of Wilf McGuinness' time in charge of first-team matters at Old Trafford.

Ure's arrival helped to stabilize United and they went unbeaten for eight games before losing at Derby in early October. The 29-year-old Scot also kept Bill Foulkes out of the team. Foulkes had played his last game for United, against Southampton at Old Trafford in United's second League defeat in August. He was 37 years old and had made 679 appearances for United. Denis Law was approaching 30 and was troubled by persistent injuries. He managed just seven appearances and one goal in the League before the end of 1969. Best and Charlton, however, remained consistently outstanding. In 1968, Charlton, then 31, had signed an eight-year contract with United, the longest in Football League history. In 1969 he was also awarded an OBE for services to football. Best, as the 1960s ended, was only 23 years old and already established as one of the world's greatest players. He showed no lack of appetite for the game.

In the final three months of 1969, United's League results continued to be mixed: five wins, five draws and four defeats. A 4-0 defeat in mid-November at Maine Road was a shocker but on 13 December they enjoyed a welcome 4-1 win at Anfield. That was a useful warm-up for the second leg of their League Cup semi-final against Manchester City four days later.

To reach that stage, United had beaten Middlesbrough, Wrexham, Burnley and Derby County. In the first leg of the semi, at Maine Road, just over 55,000 had seen United lose 2-1 in controversial circumstances.

George Best remained in excellent form for United during the 1969-70 season. However, his off-field activities were beginning to spiral out of control. He also missed the steadying presence of Busby in the dressing room and on the training-pitch.

Charlton had equalized for United after Lee's early goal for City. With two minutes remaining, Lee took a tumble under a challenge from Ure. The referee gave a penalty which Lee scored.

Bowyer extended City's aggregate lead early in the first leg of the return on 17 December. United got one back when Paul Edwards, a 22-year-old right-back, took aim from distance and hit the target. With the 64,000 crowd inflamed with derby passion, Denis Law made the aggregate 3-3 in the second half. But with just six minutes remaining, Lee took an indirect free-kick which Stepney tried to stop reaching goal. The ball spilled from his grasp and Summerbee swept it into the net. Had Stepney allowed Lee's kick to go past him it would not have stood as a goal.

In Manchester United's final match of the 1960s, on 27 December 1969, they drew 1-1 at Sunderland. Despite their average form, United could still draw the crowds – the 36,000 who assembled to watch them at Roker Park was Sunderland's biggest attendance up to then in the 1969-70 season. Best remained one of the crowd-pullers-in-chief. Playing on the left wing that day, he did not disappoint. Both he and Morgan, on the right wing, were in inventive form.

After ten minutes, Morgan's corner was flicked on by Ure. The ball sat up nicely for Kidd, who knocked it into the Sunderland net. Charlton, Burns and Crerand were in forceful form supplying Best, Morgan and Kidd in a 4-3-3 formation. United were unlucky in front of goal. Best hit the Sunderland bar with a header before Baker equalized in the second half. United had ended one of their greatest decades in something close to the style to which they had made their fans accustomed.

United finished 1969 in 11th position in the First Division, 13 points behind leaders Everton and 14 above bottom-club Sheffield Wednesday. McGuinness still had some distinguished players at his disposal. From the vantage point of New Year's Eve 1969, the 1970s could be embraced with a degree of justifiable enthusiasm. The dying decade would be looked back on with stupefaction. Unlike a certain rock singer, United had enjoyed full satisfaction from the 1960s.

(opposite page) Shay Brennan, United's regular right-back during the 1960s, did much to underpin the club's successes during the decade.

A young Bobby Charlton takes on the Tottenham Hotspur defence at White Hart Lane.

Charlton leaves the pitch after United's European Cup semi-final against Real Madrid in the Bernabeu Stadium in 1968. A memorable 3-3 draw had put United into the final.

An oft-repeated scene in the 1960s; Bobby Charlton easing away from a well-beaten defender.

Denis Law was never slow to voice his opinions to referees.

Law was an expert goal-poacher but he also scored numerous goals at the end of lengthy runs.

As United captain and goalscorer par excellence, Law really threw himself into things on the pitch.

George Best at the age of 21, watched closely by Tony Dunne and an expectant Old Trafford crowd.

A quest for perfection led Best to return to Old Trafford after training to work on his heading and his control with his left foot. The results proved positive.

(opposite)
David Sadler joined United as an amateur, aged 16, in 1962 and served the club superbly in a number of positions throughout the rest of the decade.

Matt Busby is greeted by Bill Foulkes (left) and Bobby Charlton (right) at the end of the 1968 European Cup final victory over Benfica.

Manchester United – European champions, 1968. Back row, left to right: Bill Foulkes, John Aston, Jimmy Rimmer, Alex Stepney, Alan Gowling, David Herd. Middle row: David Sadler, Tony Dunne, Shay Brennan, Pat Crerand, George Best, Francis Burns, Jack Crompton. Front row: Jim Ryan, Nobby Stiles, Denis Law, Matt Busby, Bobby Charlton, Brian Kidd, John Fitzpatrick.

Rapt delight registers on Matt Busby's face as he is pictured with a prized possession, the European Cup, club football's most distinguished trophy.

(left) Bill Foulkes, United's centre-half for almost two decades, was the cornerstone on which the club's successes were built in the 1960s.

Brian Kidd, an inside-forward, made his debut in 1967, aged 18. He was one of several home-grown talents whom United developed during the 1960s.

FACTS AND FIGURES

As a way of putting each season of the 1960s into context, this section includes a Manchester United regular eleven from each season; the full First Division League table; Manchester United's top scorer and their combined total of goals in all competitions; the result of the FA Cup final; the Footballer of the Year in England; the result of the European Cup final; and the European Footballer of the Year.

1959-60

		P	W	D	L	F	A	Pts
1	Burnley	42	24	7	11	85	61	55
2	Wolves	42	24	6	12	106	67	54
3	Tottenham	42	21	11	10	86	50	53
4	WBA	42	19	11	12	83	57	49
5	Sheff Wed	42	19	11	12	80	59	49
6	Bolton	42	20	8	14	59	51	48
7	Man United	42	19	7	16	102	80	45
8	Newcastle	42	18	8	16	82	78	44
9	Preston	42	16	12	14	79	76	44
10	Fulham	42	17	10	15	73	80	44
11	Blackpool	42	15	10	17	59	71	40
12	Leicester	42	13	13	16	66	75	39
13	Arsenal	42	15	9	18	68	80	39
14	West Ham	42	16	6	20	75	91	38
15	Man City	42	17	3	22	78	84	37
16	Everton	42	13	11	18	73	78	37
17	Blackburn	42	16	5	21	60	70	37
18	Chelsea	42	14	9	19	76	91	37
19	Birmingham	42	13	10	19	63	80	36
20	Nottm Forest	42	13	9	20	50	74	35
21	Leeds	42	12	10	20	65	92	34
22	Luton	42	9	12	21	50	73	30

1959-60

Manchester United first eleven: Gregg, Foulkes, Carolan, Setters, Cope, Brennan, Bradley, Quixall, Viollet, Charlton, Scanlon.

Leading scorer - Dennis Viollet - 32 goals

FA Cup Final - Wolverhampton Wanderers 3 Blackburn Rovers 0, Wembley Stadium, attendance 100,000

Footballer of the Year - Bill Slater (Wolverhampton Wanderers)

European Cup Final - Real Madrid 7 Eintracht Frankfurt 3, Glasgow, attendance 135,000

European Footballer of the Year - Luis Suarez (Barcelona)

1960-61

		P	W	D	L	F	A	Pts
1	Tottenham	42	31	4	7	115	55	66
2	Sheff Wed	42	23	12	7	78	47	58
3	Wolves	42	25	7	10	103	75	57
4	Burnley	42	22	7	13	102	77	51
5	Everton	42	22	6	14	87	69	50
6	Leicester	42	18	9	15	87	70	45
7	Man United	42	18	9	15	88	76	45
8	Blackpool	42	15	13	14	77	76	43
9	Aston Villa	42	17	9	16	78	77	43
10	WBA	42	18	5	19	67	71	41
11	Arsenal	42	15	11	16	77	85	41
12	Chelsea	42	15	7	20	98	100	37
13	Man City	42	13	11	18	79	90	37
14	Nottm Forest	42	14	9	19	62	78	37
15	Cardiff	42	13	11	18	60	85	37
16	West Ham	42	13	10	19	77	88	36
17	Fulham	42	14	8	20	72	95	36
18	Bolton	42	12	11	19	58	73	35
19	Birmingham	42	14	6	22	62	84	34
20	Blackpool	42	12	9	21	68	73	33
21	Newcastle	42	11	10	21	86	109	32
22	Preston	42	10	10	22	43	71	30

1960-61

Manchester United first eleven: Gregg, Brennan, Cantwell, Setters, Foulkes, Nicholson, Giles, Quixall, Dawson, Pearson, Charlton.

Leading scorer - Bobby Charlton - 20 goals

FA Cup Final - Tottenham Hotspur 2 Leicester City 0, Wembley Stadium, attendance 100,000

Footballer of the Year - Danny Blanchflower (Tottenham Hotspur)

European Cup Final - Benfica 3 Barcelona 2, Berne, attendance 28,000

European Footballer of the Year - Omar Sivori (Juventus)

1961-62

Manchester United first eleven: Gaskell, Brennan, Dunne, Stiles, Foulkes, Setters, Quixall, Giles, Herd, Lawton, Charlton.
Leading scorer - David Herd - 17 goals
FA Cup Final - Tottenham Hotspur 3 Burnley 1, Wembley Stadium, attendance 100,000
Footballer of the Year - Jimmy Adamson (Burnley)
European Cup Final - Benfica 5 Real Madrid 3, Amsterdam, attendance 65,000
European Footballer of the Year - Josef Masopust (Dukla Prague)

1961-62

		P	W	D	L	F	A	Pts
1	Ipswich	42	24	8	10	93	67	56
2	Burnley	42	21	11	10	101	67	53
3	Tottenham	42	21	10	11	88	69	52
4	Everton	42	20	11	11	88	54	51
5	Sheff United	42	19	9	14	61	69	47
6	Sheff Wed	42	20	60	16	72	58	46
7	Aston Villa	42	18	8	16	65	56	44
8	West Ham	42	17	10	15	76	82	44
9	WBA	42	15	13	14	83	67	43
10	Arsenal	42	16	11	15	71	72	43
11	Bolton	42	16	10	16	62	66	42
12	Man City	42	17	7	18	78	81	41
13	Blackpool	42	15	11	16	70	75	41
14	Leicester	42	17	6	19	72	71	40
15	Man United	42	15	9	18	72	75	39
16	Blackburn	42	14	11	17	50	58	39
17	Birmingham	42	14	10	18	65	81	38
18	Wolves	42	13	10	19	73	86	36
19	Nottm Forest	42	13	10	19	63	79	36
20	Fulham	42	13	7	22	66	74	33
21	Cardiff	42	9	14	19	50	81	32
22	Chelsea	42	9	10	23	63	94	28

1962-63

Manchester United first eleven: Gregg, Brennan, Cantwell, Crerand, Foulkes, Setters, Giles, Quixall, Herd, Law, Charlton.
Leading scorer - Denis Law - 30 goals
FA Cup Final - Manchester United 3 Leicester City 1, Wembley Stadium, attendance 100,000
Footballer of the Year - Stanley Matthews (Stoke City)
European Cup Final - Milan 2 Benfica 1, Wembley Stadium, attendance 45,000
European Footballer of the Year - Lev Yashin (Moscow Dynamo)

1962-63

		P	W	D	L	F	A	Pts
1	Everton	42	25	11	6	84	82	61
2	Tottenham	42	23	9	10	111	62	55
3	Burnley	42	22	10	10	78	57	54
4	Leicester	42	20	12	10	79	53	52
5	Wolves	42	20	10	12	93	65	50
6	Sheff Wed	42	19	10	13	77	63	48
7	Arsenal	42	18	10	14	86	77	46
8	Liverpool	42	17	10	15	71	59	44
9	Nottm Forest	42	17	10	15	67	69	44
10	Sheff United	44	16	12	14	58	60	44
11	Blackburn	42	15	12	15	79	71	42
12	West Ham	42	14	12	16	73	69	40
13	Blackpool	42	13	14	15	58	64	40
14	WBA	42	16	7	19	71	79	39
15	Aston Villa	42	15	8	19	62	68	38
16	Fulham	42	14	10	18	50	71	38
17	Ipswich	42	12	11	19	59	78	35
18	Bolton	42	15	5	22	55	75	35
19	Man United	42	12	10	20	67	81	34
20	Birmingham	42	10	13	19	63	90	33
21	Man City	42	10	11	21	58	102	31
22	Leyton Orient	42	6	9	27	37	81	21

1963-64

Manchester United first eleven: Gaskell, Dunne, Cantwell, Crerand, Foulkes, Setters, Herd, Chisnall, Sadler, Law, Charlton.
Leading scorer - Denis Law - 46 goals
FA Cup Final - West Ham United 3 Preston North End 2, Wembley Stadium, attendance 100,000
Footballer of the Year - Bobby Moore (West Ham United)
European Cup Final - Internazionale 3 Real Madrid 1, Vienna, attendance 74,000
European Footballer of the Year - Denis Law (Manchester United)

1963-64

		P	W	D	L	F	A	Pts
1	Liverpool	42	26	5	11	92	45	57
2	Man United	42	23	7	12	80	62	53
3	Everton	42	21	10	11	84	64	52
4	Tottenham	42	22	7	16	97	81	51
5	Chelsea	42	20	10	12	72	56	50
6	Sheff Wed	42	19	11	12	84	67	49
7	Blackburn	42	18	10	14	89	65	46
8	Arsenal	42	17	11	14	90	82	45
9	Burnley	42	17	10	15	71	64	44
10	WBA	42	16	11	15	70	61	43
11	Leicester	42	16	11	15	61	58	43
12	Sheff United	42	16	11	15	61	64	43
13	Nottm Forest	42	16	9	17	64	68	41
14	West Ham	42	14	12	16	69	74	40
15	Fulham	42	13	13	16	58	65	39
16	Wolves	42	12	15	15	70	80	39
17	Stoke	42	14	10	18	77	78	38
18	Blackpool	42	13	9	20	52	73	35
19	Aston Villa	42	11	12	19	62	71	34
20	Birmingham	42	11	7	24	54	92	29
21	Bolton	42	10	8	24	48	80	28
22	Ipswich	42	9	7	26	56	121	25

1964-65

		P	W	D	L	F	A	Pts
1	Man United	42	26	9	7	89	39	61
2	Leeds	42	26	9	7	83	52	61
3	Chelsea	42	24	8	10	89	54	56
4	Everton	42	17	15	10	69	60	49
5	Nottm Forest	42	17	13	12	71	67	47
6	Tottenham	42	19	7	16	87	71	45
7	Liverpool	42	17	10	15	67	73	44
8	Sheff Wed	42	16	11	15	57	55	43
9	West Ham	42	19	4	19	82	71	42
10	Blackburn	42	16	10	16	83	79	42
11	Stoke	42	16	10	16	67	66	42
12	Burnley	42	16	10	16	70	70	42
13	Arsenal	42	17	7	18	69	75	41
14	WBA	42	13	13	16	70	65	39
15	Sunderland	42	14	9	19	64	74	37
16	Aston Villa	42	16	5	21	57	82	37
17	Blackpool	42	12	11	19	67	78	35
18	Leicester	42	11	13	18	69	85	35
19	Sheff United	42	12	11	19	50	64	35
20	Fulham	42	11	12	19	60	78	34
21	Wolves	42	13	4	25	59	89	30
22	Birmingham	42	8	11	23	64	96	27

1964-65

Manchester United first eleven: P Dunne, Brennan, A Dunne, Crerand, Foulkes, Stiles, Connelly, Charlton, Herd, Law, Best.

Leading scorer - Denis Law - 39 goals

FA Cup Final - Liverpool 2 Leeds United 1, Wembley Stadium, attendance 100,000

Footballer of the Year - Bobby Collins (Leeds United)

European Cup Final - Internazionale 1 Benfica 0, Milan, attendance 80,000

European Footballer of the Year - Eusebio (Benfica)

1965-66

		P	W	D	L	F	A	Pts
1	Liverpool	42	26	9	7	79	34	61
2	Leeds	42	23	9	10	79	38	55
3	Burnley	42	24	7	11	79	47	55
4	Man United	42	18	15	9	84	59	51
5	Chelsea	42	22	7	13	65	53	51
6	WBA	42	19	12	11	91	69	50
7	Leicester	42	21	7	14	80	65	49
8	Tottenham	42	16	12	14	75	66	44
9	Sheff United	42	16	11	15	56	59	43
10	Stoke	42	15	12	15	65	64	42
11	Everton	42	15	11	16	56	62	41
12	West Ham	42	15	9	18	70	83	39
13	Blackpool	42	14	9	19	55	65	37
14	Arsenal	42	12	13	17	62	75	37
15	Newcastle	42	14	9	19	50	63	37
16	Aston Villa	42	15	6	21	69	80	36
17	Sheff Wed	42	14	8	20	56	66	36
18	Nottm Forest	42	14	8	20	56	72	36
19	Sunderland	42	14	8	20	51	72	36
20	Fulham	42	14	7	21	67	85	35
21	Northampton	42	10	13	19	55	92	33
22	Blackburn	42	8	4	30	57	88	20

1965-66

Manchester United first eleven: Gregg, Brennan, Dunne, Crerand, Foulkes, Stiles, Best, Law, Charlton, Herd, Connelly.

Leading scorer - David Herd - 31 goals

FA Cup Final - Everton 3 Sheffield Wednesday 2, Wembley Stadium, attendance 100,000

Footballer of the Year - Bobby Charlton (Manchester United)

European Cup Final - Real Madrid 2 Partizan Belgrade 1, Brussels, attendance 55,000

European Footballer of the Year - Bobby Charlton (Manchester United)

1966-67

		P	W	D	L	F	A	Pts
1	Man United	42	24	12	6	84	45	60
2	Nottm Forest	42	23	10	9	64	41	56
3	Tottenham	42	24	8	10	71	48	56
4	Leeds	42	22	11	9	62	42	55
5	Liverpool	42	19	13	10	64	47	51
6	Everton	42	19	10	13	65	46	48
7	Arsenal	42	16	14	12	58	47	46
8	Leicester	42	18	8	16	78	71	44
9	Chelsea	42	15	14	13	67	62	44
10	Sheff United	42	16	10	16	52	59	42
11	Sheff Wed	42	14	13	15	56	47	41
12	Stoke	42	17	7	18	63	58	41
13	WBA	42	16	7	19	77	73	39
14	Burnley	42	15	9	18	66	76	39
15	Man City	42	12	15	15	43	52	39
16	West Ham	42	14	8	20	80	84	36
17	Sunderland	42	14	8	20	58	72	36
18	Fulham	42	11	12	19	71	83	34
19	Southampton	42	14	6	22	74	92	34
20	Newcastle	42	12	9	21	39	81	33
21	Aston Villa	42	11	7	24	54	85	29
22	Blackpool	42	6	9	27	41	76	21

1966-67

Manchester United first eleven: Stepney, Dunne, Noble, Crerand, Foulkes, Stiles, Best, Law, Sadler, Charlton, Aston.

Leading scorer - Denis Law - 25 goals

FA Cup Final - Tottenham Hotspur 2 Chelsea 1, Wembley Stadium, attendance 100,000

Footballer of the Year - Jackie Charlton (Leeds United)

European Cup Final - Celtic 2 Internazionale 1, Lisbon, attendance 56,000

European Footballer of the Year - Florian Albert (Ferencvaros)

1967-68

Manchester United first eleven: Stepney, Dunne, Burns, Crerand, Foulkes, Stiles, Best, Kidd, Charlton, Law, Aston.

Leading scorer - George Best - 32 goals

FA Cup Final - West Bromwich Albion 1 Everton 0, Wembley Stadium, attendance 100,000

Footballer of the Year - George Best (Manchester United)

European Cup Final - Manchester United 4 Benfica 1, Wembley Stadium, attendance 100,000

European Footballer of the Year - George Best (Manchester United)

1967-68

		P	W	D	L	F	A	Pts
1	Man City	42	26	6	10	86	43	58
2	Man United	42	24	8	10	89	55	56
3	Liverpool	42	22	11	9	71	40	55
4	Leeds	42	22	9	11	71	41	53
5	Everton	42	23	6	13	67	40	52
6	Chelsea	42	18	12	12	62	68	48
7	Tottenham	42	19	9	14	70	59	47
8	WBA	42	17	12	13	75	62	46
9	Arsenal	42	17	10	15	60	56	44
10	Newcastle	42	13	15	14	54	67	41
11	Nottm Forest	42	14	11	17	52	64	39
12	West Ham	42	14	10	18	73	69	38
13	Leicester	42	13	12	17	64	69	38
14	Burnley	42	14	10	18	64	71	38
15	Sunderland	42	13	11	18	51	61	37
16	Southampton	42	13	11	18	66	83	37
17	Wolves	42	14	8	20	66	75	36
18	Stoke	42	14	7	21	50	73	35
19	Sheff Wed	42	11	12	19	51	63	34
20	Coventry	42	9	15	18	51	71	33
21	Sheff United	42	11	10	21	49	70	32
22	Fulham	42	10	7	25	56	98	27

1968-69

Manchester United first eleven: Stepney, Fitzpatrick, Dunne, Crerand, James, Stiles, Morgan, Kidd, Charlton, Law, Best.

Leading scorer - Denis Law - 30 goals

FA Cup Final - Manchester City 1 Leicester City 0, Wembley Stadium, attendance 100,000

Footballer of the Year - Dave Mackay (Derby County) shared with Tony Book (Manchester City)

European Cup Final - Milan 4 Ajax 1, Madrid, attendance 50,000

European Footballer of the Year - Gianni Rivera (Milan)

1968-69

		P	W	D	L	F	A	Pts
1	Leeds	42	27	13	2	66	26	67
2	Liverpool	42	25	11	6	63	24	61
3	Everton	42	21	15	6	77	36	57
4	Arsenal	42	22	12	8	56	27	56
5	Chelsea	42	20	10	12	73	53	50
6	Tottenham	42	14	17	11	61	51	45
7	Southampton	42	16	13	13	57	48	45
8	West Ham	42	13	18	11	66	50	44
9	Newcastle	42	15	14	13	61	55	44
10	WBA	42	16	11	15	64	67	43
11	Man United	42	15	12	15	57	53	42
12	Ipswich	42	15	11	16	59	60	41
13	Man City	42	15	10	17	64	55	40
14	Burnley	42	15	9	18	55	82	39
15	Sheff Wed	42	10	16	16	41	54	36
16	Wolves	42	10	15	17	41	58	35
17	Sunderland	42	11	12	19	43	67	34
18	Nottm Forest	42	10	13	19	45	57	33
19	Stoke	42	9	15	18	40	63	33
20	Coventry	42	10	11	21	46	64	31
21	Leicester	42	9	12	21	39	68	30
22	QPR	42	4	10	28	39	95	18

1969-70

Manchester United first eleven: Stepney, Edwards, Dunne, Crerand, Ure, Sadler, Morgan, Sartori, Charlton, Kidd, Best.

Leading scorer - George Best - 23 goals

FA Cup Final - Chelsea 2 Leeds United 1, Old Trafford, attendance 62,078 (after 2-2 draw at Wembley)

Footballer of the Year - Billy Bremner (Leeds United)

European Cup Final - Feyenoord 2 Celtic 1, Milan, attendance 50,000

European Footballer of the Year - Gerd Muller (Bayern Munich)

1969-70

		P	W	D	L	F	A	Pts
1	Everton	42	29	8	5	72	34	66
2	Leeds	42	21	15	6	84	49	57
3	Chelsea	42	21	13	8	70	50	55
4	Derby	42	22	9	11	64	37	53
5	Liverpool	42	20	11	11	65	42	51
6	Coventry	42	19	11	12	58	48	49
7	Newcastle	42	17	13	12	57	35	47
8	Man United	42	14	17	11	66	61	45
9	Stoke	42	15	15	12	56	52	45
10	Man City	42	16	11	15	55	48	43
11	Tottenham	42	17	9	16	54	55	43
12	Arsenal	42	12	18	12	51	49	42
13	Wolves	42	12	16	14	55	57	40
14	Burnley	42	12	15	15	56	61	39
15	Nottm Forest	42	10	18	14	50	71	38
16	WBA	42	14	9	19	58	66	37
17	West Ham	42	12	12	18	51	60	36
18	Ipswich	42	10	11	21	40	63	31
19	Southampton	42	6	17	19	46	67	29
20	Crystal Palace	42	6	15	21	34	68	27
21	Sunderland	42	6	14	22	30	68	26
22	Sheff Wed	42	8	9	25	40	71	25

Selected Bibliography

The Hamlyn Illustrated History of Manchester United 1878-1996
David Meek and Tom Tyrell, Reed International books Limited, London,
1996.

The United Alphabet, Garth Dykes, ACL Colour Print & Polar
Publishing (UK) Ltd, Leicester 1994.

The International Football Book No. 3, edited by Stratton Smith
Souvenir Press, London 1961.

Father of Football, David Miller, Pavilion Books Limited, London, 1971
& 1994.

A Strange Kind of Glory, Eamon Dunphy. Mandarin Paperbacks,
London, 1992.

Old Trafford, Theatre of Dreams, Iain McCartney, Yore Publications,
Harefield, Middlesex, 1996.

Picture Acknowledgement

The memorabilia items on the cover were photographed by Peter Letts.

Allsport: front cover bottom, 58, 72 bottom, 85 top, 86 middle, 87 top, 89
top, 90 frontcover top; Allsport Historical Collection: 8; Allsport/Hulton
Deutsch: right, iv top, 9, 13, 18, 23 middle left, 24 middle left and bottom
left, 29, 44 top, 51, 52 53 both, 54, 62, 63 bottom 67, 73 middle, 74 bottom,
81; Colorsport: iv bottom, v, 15, 16, 17, 20, 37, 43, 45, 46 both, 57, 61, 63 top
64, 80, 82, 83, 84, 85 bottom, 87 bottom, 88, 91 top; Hulton Getty/Allsport:
10; Keystone Collection: 24 middle right; Manchester Evening News, photo
by Peter Letts 24 top; MSI/Allsport 66; Popperfoto: front cover top left, 7,
11, 23 top right and bottom right, 25, 27, 31, 33 both, 39, 44 bottom, 48, 72
top and middle, 73 top and bottom, 74 top, 77, 78 all, 85 middle, 86 top and
bottom, 98 bottom, 91 bottom; Rex Features: 36.